To Jessica,

I love you! I am so proud of you! You inspire me with your courage & persistence. Keep going & I can't wait for our leadership!

Love,
Mrs. LaPhenie

All rights reserved. No part of this book may be reproduced or transmitted in any form or by any means without written permission from the author.

ISBN-13:978-1546587330

Printed in the United States.

ADDICTED

"How My Addiction Led Me To My Destiny"

"Destiny Driven LC"

This Book is Dedicated to:

My Mother Loretta Woods and Father Leroy Bridges

Aunts (Joyce, Winnifred, Pearl) and Uncles (Wendell, Henry),

Leroy, Louis, Lawrence, Lawanna, Lamar, Bernella, Sheila, Kenneth, Sharon, Kevin

Niyia (Karl), Sharmayne (Romondo), Sherman III (Virginia)

Darrelle and Caleb (You make my heart sing)

To my Devoted Husband, Thanks for the numerous and unselfish sacrifices it took to make this happen! I Love you eternally! The Cloyd Family!

To my Cousins (All of You)

Toni Mays my dearest friend and GOD given sister.

Thank you to the Village that helped raise me, where would I be without you?

Special Thanks to The LCADA WAY family, you allowed me to grow in ways that words could never describe. Thank You!!!

Pastor Karious and Momma Queen McDaniel I Love You!

Dr. Melvin and Sis. Beverly Woodard and Mt. Zion Baptist Church Thank You! The Voices of Praise

Apostle Brian and Pastor Holly Wade, I am grateful for you and your children!

Pastor Marilyn Parker Jeffries, Bro Abe and New Creation Baptist Church you are wonderful!

Joyce Pleasant and Sandra Scott, I Adore You!

In Memory of:

Mollie Adams (Granny)

Diane and Kenneth Caldwell (Aunt and Uncle)

Antoinette Thorton

Vera Whitsett

Nona Burney

Charlie and Annie Sea

Steadman Pleasant

Gracie White and Carol White

Bill Finley

Crystal Smith and Velma Burnette

Loretta Lee, Michael Ruebensaal, & Lewis Johnson

Chapter Titles

1. "The Little Girl"

2. "My Faith Foundation"

3. "Growing Up in The Hood"

4. "My First Love is Singing and Going to Church"

5. "School and The Big House"

6. "Being A Teenagers Can be Challenging Years"

7. "Fashion, Make-Up, and Hair"

8. "I Began to Experiment" "Music, Boys, and What's that Smell"

9. "Don't Turn Your Back on A Golden Opportunity"

10. "Mommie Don't' Know Nothing"

11. "Looking for Love in All the Wrong Places"

12. "What Happened? How Did I Get Here?"

13. "If you need help…Ask"

14. "My daughter and I"

15. "Beauty School and Music"

16. "New Opportunities and New Adventures"

17. "Trying to Find My "Fit" in Life!"

18. "My first Marriage"

19. "Love has Everything to do with it!"

20. "College Park Georgia"

21. "Returning to Cleveland, Ohio"

22. "Living A lie"

23. "East Cleveland"

24. "The Nightmare Begins"

25. "Recovery"

26. "Lorain, Ohio"

27. "Alcohol and Drug Treatment, AA meetings and Church"

28. "Returning to My First Love, God"

29. "Lord Please Restore Me"

30. Staying Focused through Prayer!!!

31. "Another Level"

32. "Reunited"

33. "My Life Today"

Foreword

LaPhenie Cloyd is a special woman with an amazing story. I know her story very well because I share a portion of it with her. Through the grace of God, I happened to be there as she began to change into the God-fearing woman she has truly become. You see, I was her pastor. I was one of the trusted voices in her life. But I can assure you, I was not a willing participant (initially) as LaPhenie struggled with her addiction and the various outcomes of addiction in her life. But she had a relentless inner desire to go another way and God knitted us together.

When I first met LaPhenie in the mid 1990's she was in Lorain, Ohio, staying at a transition home next to my church. She had made friends with the church secretary and asked often to come into the sanctuary. She had a simple desire – she wanted to pray - and frequently asked for someone to do it with her. My secretary kept pushing me to pray with her, even when she was "high." Joyfully, a change occurred. It was to my shame though, because I thought she was "too far" gone. God is so good!!! And He is forgiving, for my sake.

In the days, weeks, months, and years ahead, LaPhenie taught me so much about the saving power of God. Once she was restored to health – physically and most importantly spiritually – she brought one person after another to Christ. At one point, LaPhenie was responsible for an untold number of members coming to know Christ in our church. She had become an amazingly powerful witness for Jesus Christ, and she still is to this day as she preaches the Gospel. Even after losing her family and children, God restored her children and gave her a new husband that is on fire for the Lord.

I am extremely pleased and proud to write this piece and share a glimpse of what I know about this remarkable woman of God. Her children, especially her daughters, are every bit as powerful as she is. This book, *"How My Addiction Led Me To My Destiny"* is worth your time to read. It provides insight and understanding of one woman's journey through the darkness of addiction. I recommend this book, even more so, because it shows the power of God to lift anyone from the deepest depths to the highest heights of life.

May the grace of our Lord and Savior Jesus Christ be as real and powerful in your life!

Dr. Melvin J. Woodard III

Pastor and Founder, New Salem MBC

Being asked to write the forward for LaPhenie's book is a great honor. It has caused me to reflect on the importance of the journey that those suffering from addiction must travel.

I entered the field of addiction treatment 39 years ago, with no idea or intention to making this my career. In 1978, I was working with youth who were diagnosed as emotionally disturbed in a residential treatment center. These young men would be in residential treatment anywhere from one to three years and receive their schooling on campus and I would be responsible for the treatment/therapy that they and their families would receive.
What became apparent through my work is that half of those that I was treating were getting better and half were not. This was a professional dilemma that I struggled with a great deal. While in graduate school and through my internship I had read a book by Vernon Johnson, founder of the Johnson Institute in Minneapolis Minnesota. He wrote about a concept of chemical dependency. I wanted to explore this more and the center was willing to send me to Johnson Institute for training. What I discovered there was that the half of my adolescents who were not getting better were either chemically dependent or their parents were chemically dependent and I began to put together interventions to begin dealing with their illness.

Now this is before there were addiction treatment centers in every community. If you were to get treatment you would have to go to one of a very few and usually far away from home. Then in the early 1980's we saw a proliferation of chemical dependency treatment centers open up in every community. It seemed that every hospital opened-up a treatment unit. Because I was one of the few in the area to receive training I was recruited by several hospitals to join their treatment team. It was nice being recruited and so I thought I would accept a position with Lakeland Institute. My thinking at that time was I will accept the position, stay a few years and it will look good on my resume and then I will return to working in mental health. Well that was 37 years ago, and I truly could not imagine working in any other field. This is a field where miracles do happen!

LaPhenie's journey is testimonial to that miraculous journey from the onset of use and abuse, through the devastation of the addiction, to the miracle of recovery. I am so blessed to know LaPhenie and to have seen her continue to touch and shape the lives of young people struggling with this disease.

Tom Stuber-CEO-The LCADA Way

The path to alcohol and drug addiction is not the same for everyone. But in each case the pain/boredom/guilt/fear/sadness/shame is at least initially reduced by chemicals that quickly impact the brain's pleasure centers. What other action can we find that has such rapid action and feels so good? And better yet it doesn't require another person's participation or love!

The author's frank and personal story is both heartbreaking and uplifting. The author had positive early grounding in an exceptionally strong family supplemented by the very strong support of her church family. These experiences along with her involvement with music seem to have provided her from earliest childhood a life-saving identity of intrinsic worth as a human being. This was enhanced by the very personal relationship she experienced with a caring and living God instilled by her powerful, loving and exceptional "granny".

Conversely, the abandonment by a parent in childhood usually leaves a hole in the heart which can produce dysfunction later in a person's identity and relationships. This seems true for the author as she describes in Chapter one of her book. Her father's reappearance into her life when she was at her lowest point is significant. It's not unlikely that much of her destructive relationships with men were influenced by her early childhood internalization of the meaning of her father's abandonment and unconscious attempts to regain his love. In any case her search for love, relationships with men, with the physical and emotional abuse she suffered as a consequence violated the self she had so well cultivated as a child and young woman. This violation led to the temporary destruction of self during her years of addiction we see so clearly described in this book. I often marvel at how some individuals can return to quality and productive lives from the depths of terribly painful periods of emotional distress while others cannot escape a continuous sad and miserable life. While there remain many mysteries to this question I think this story helps us understand the importance to the author of early childhood love, internalization of a loving God, and powerful family support for deep positive identity formation.

In her moment of deepest despair and hopelessness the author was somehow able to go deep into herself and find in her human history that personal meaning and worth, that little girl's granny which she had temporarily lost. Her God, her family, her church, her music and most important of all her human dignity and self-worth that she had felt so strongly in her youth. This is a powerful first-person story of family, pain, addiction and survival and the strength of a "Loving Village" that made recovery possible.

Charles Ross PhD, Psychologist

Introduction

What is Truth? Truth is the real facts about something or someone.

At some point, I realized I must face the plain old naked truth about who I am, whether I like it or not, in order for me to change things in my life.

The truth is, I have finally begun to accept and receive peace about my own personal truths.

The truth is that the very thing that caused my destruction and bondage is the very thing that brought me life! The truth is the very thing that caused me shame, humiliation and disgrace, eventually led to my freedom.

The characteristics in me that are flawed, inappropriate and destructive, God have found a way to use them for my good. By turning them from bad habits to useful skills that I can use for a good purpose! In other words, what once was a liability to me is now an asset! Therefore, I wrote this book to assure you that "You Can Change your Future."

I had to face the fact that people are afraid of what they do not understand! How could they understand my reality, when they have never walked a single step in my shoes? My goal and purpose for sharing my story is to give those who share or have shared my struggle, new hope! This brings me to the start or beginning of my story. So, here's to the Good, the Bad, and the Ugly side of Me!

"I have told you these things, so that in me you may have peace. In this world, you will have trouble. But take heart, because I have overcome the world" (John 16:33).

Even when things get difficult and hard to understand, deal with, or cope with, we have a friend named JESUS who will help us carry our heavy Load.

Chapter 1

"The Little Girl"

Do children really get a choice in which their parents or families will be? No, not at all! We are born into our unique situations for a reason and only God has the Answer to that question.

I was born January 5, 1962 to Lloyd and Linda Blair. I was named after my great grandma because I was born on her Birthday. Her name was Tanese. My dad named us all with the letter L, and therefore, my name is LaTanese Janet Blair. My mom chose Janet because that is her oldest sister's name and she is quite awesome. Growing up, I was often told that my name was unique and I liked that. It made me feel like I had something special that belonged only to me. Although, I never had the opportunity to meet my great grandmother, I often wonder what kind of person she was. What did she look like? What color was she and did we have anything else in common besides our birthdate and our name? Anyhow, I guess I will never know because she died before I got to know her. I resolved that just being named after her was enough for me and I determined to become the best LaTanese I could be.

As a little girl, my mom told me that she was my mom and therefore, that makes her my boss, and she was in charge of me 24hours a day, seven days a week. She paid the bills and therefore, she made the rules. I am number five in my sibling birth order and the youngest child between my mom and dad. My dad did not raise me, therefore, he was not there to assist me in growing up. This hurt me badly. I have a memory of my dad at age three. He brought my brothers, sister, and I some Hershey chocolate bars. That is my last memory of seeing my father as a child. I never forgot him and I longed for him my whole life. When my parents got divorced, my mom remarried and had two more children. My dad remarried and had four more children. Between my mom and dad, there are eleven of us. I have three older brothers (Lloyd, Lamont, and Leonard) and one older sister (Laurene). I also have one younger brother (Landon) and sister (Barbara) by my mom. I also have two younger brothers (Karl and Kenton) and two younger sisters (Sherry and Sheryl) by my dad and his second wife (Joyce), whom I did not meet until way later in my life. As you can see, both of my parents really love children. I was always taught growing up as child that family and friends are all we have. I guess that is why my family and friends mean the world to me.

"Flashback"

"Alright class! Settle down! As I point to you please stand and say your name and age. My name is LaTanese Janet Blair and I am five years old! Taking my seat, I began to wonder "Who am I?"

"I think this was the turning point in my life that led to my becoming "Destiny Driven"

I set out as a child to find my purpose in life and the reason that I was created, so I could live my life to the fullest of my potential.

Chapter 2

"My Faith Foundation"

I remember my granny going to church and taking our entire family with her. Throughout my childhood and earliest memories my family has always been in church. My granny made sure that we knew who GOD was, why he created us, and what our purpose here on earth was as the children of GOD. My granny was a firm believer that a "family that prays together, stays together." She looked after all the children in our neighborhood and everyone called her momma, mother, granny, or friend. In our community and abroad, she was known as "Missionary Millie Allgood. We always had strangers at our family dinners, celebrations, and holidays. She had the heart of GOD evidenced by her always giving to those in need. She was a noble woman of great character and well respected in the community. She sat in the company of kings and walked in the community among common people.

My granny was a prayer warrior and she prayed about everything. People called her for advice about everything from A to Z.

She would light her prayer candles and sit alone and pray for hours. I believe this is the reason I love candles and why I pray so much each day. My granny had a direct line to GOD and she taught me that God was never too busy to hear me pray. She also taught me to believe that God answers prayer. I remember being a little girl and watching my grandma sing, play organ, direct the church choir, record records at the studio (I still have some of her recordings), and feed the hungry in our community and all over the world. I remember when I was a little girl and my granny traveled to Africa with her church. I wanted to go, but was told I was too little to travel with her. All I knew was I was going to miss her and I cried myself to sleep each night until she returned home. She was my "Shero." Whenever it was raining outside with thunder and lightning, my granny would have all her grandchildren sit down and be quiet because she said GOD was at work and God was to be respected. She never allowed us to play with God or use his name in vain.

My granny was my life and as a child, my whole world revolved around my granny. I was always around her and she took me everywhere she went, except to the BB King Concerts that she attended every year. I remember at eight years old my granny getting so sick that the doctor had to make a house call to check on my granny because she was too weak to go to the hospital. The nerve of them! Putting me out of the room while this stranger tended to my granny. Truth be told, I was scared to death. I stood right outside her bedroom door and listened until the doctor, my mom, and aunt came out. When they did, I snuck inside and hid in the corner of her room and began to cry. There lay my granny still and quiet and she said "LaTanese" is that you? Why are you crying? I replied that I was scared that she was going to die. She assured me that she was going to be all right because Jesus was going to heal her. She told me to stop crying and pray for Jesus to make her well. And guess what? I prayed and Jesus healed my granny! Jesus became my best friend. After that, it was on. I made sure that everyone, everywhere I went knew about my best friend Jesus! After witnessing granny's supernatural healing, whatever granny said was law.

"Some things we experience in life are pivotal for us and these events become life changing to us as we continue our journey through life"

I was no longer the same after witnessing the healing of my grandmother. Like Ruth in the Bible, my granny became my Naomi and her GOD became my GOD.

Chapter 3

"Growing Up in The Hood"

Why was my skin so dark? Since my earliest memories, I was always called "the black girl." My brothers and sisters, cousins, and friends always reminded me about how dark I was. They would say I was cute, but I was dark. I was talented, but I was dark. I could sing, but I was dark. Not to mention, I grew up in an era when being light skinned was always right, the best, and the first choice. Anyhow, this is the truth I perceived as a child. As I began to grow up, I came to understand that my dark skin was a gift from GOD because this is what my granny told me. My granny always told me that I am beautiful, and of course my granny was always right.

My Mommie was beautiful. She was shapely and hard a big bright smile that could light up a room. Nobody messed with my momma. She always had the last say in our house. My momma was clean and respectful and that is the way she taught us to be. We didn't have a lot of money, but we had a lot of love and we were taught morals. My momma was a seamstress by trade and she was the best at doing hair. She could make anybody beautiful from head to toe. She was a professional seamstress and sewed for our entire family and most of our neighborhood friends. I remember momma making velvet dresses for all the girls in our family one Christmas. Mines were maroon and my sisters were hunter green. She also was excellent at doing hair. My sister Laurene had long thick hair and I always wanted my hair like hers. Although, my hair was short, momma always made me look really pretty. When I was older, momma would say "You got all the talent; you can buy you some hair." Momma was funny too!

Momma taught us to speak when entering a room and we were to respect older people period or else there would be consequences to pay. You see, back in the day, people used to look out for one another's children in the neighborhood. Yes, that meant you could get a whooping by anybody grown your momma gave permission to and you better not back talk. Aunties, uncles, teachers, church members, and baby sitters all had to be respected and obeyed. We even had to stand and give our seats to older people on the bus or even in a crowded room. Back in the day community practiced the motto "It takes a village to raise a child."

I truly Thank GOD for the unsung Heroes and Shero's in our neighborhood. Thank you All for being there for me.

People today call them nosy neighbors, but if anything happened in the neighborhood, the neighborhood watch was always on patrol and would report it to the proper authorities.

Chapter 4

"My First Love is Singing and going to Church"

I remember going to my grannie's church with my family at age five and my cousin Justin was there who was three years old. My granny began singing "Yes Jesus Loves Me" and he knew the words too. I remember thinking how did he know the words to that song and I didn't? Who taught him that song? I should know the words too, especially since I was two years older than him. Well, I was about to fix that. I went to my granny the next day and asked her to teach me the words to "Yes Jesus Loves Me" and I haven't stopped singing since that day.

I began going to Unity Baptist Church with my aunt Pam and uncle Deacon John when I was eight years old. I was baptized at the age of nine years old. We went to church all week long. On Sunday, we went to Sunday School, Morning and afternoon services. We went to prayer meeting on Wednesday, choir practice on Thursday, and usher board meeting on Saturday. We even went to church for special services on Friday night. I always made sure my chores were done so I could attend church. My pastor and his wife Rev. and Sis. Micha took me under their wing and I became friends with their children (Kory, Kyle, and Karen) I began spending weekends over their house. I even got into trouble around age 11 when I was over their house and Rev. Micha had to "whoop me. Who talks to someone for a long time and then whoops them? He even gave me the old "this is going to hurt me more than its going to hurt you" speech." Well, you can bet that never happened again. My Sunday School teacher was Nina Barnes. I believe she prayed some Sunday's that I did not attend Sunday School. I would sometimes need redirecting in class. Not to mention, sometimes a punishment would follow. I thank God for Sis. Nina because she hung in there with me until I got it right. She became so precious to me and when she died I stood at her coffin apologizing for being so bad in Sunday School. Her Sister Joyce hugged me and said, "don't worry about that Tanese, you were always one of her special children."

Boy, did we think back and have a good laugh!

I had accurate knowledge about attending different churches because my granny's church was Pentecostal, my mother was raised Methodist and I was Baptist. It did not matter to me what religion it was because my granny told me there is "One" same GOD who ruled this World. Everything in it belongs to him. The only thing different about religions was that people did not worship God the same. I remember that granny had all her grandchildren sing in a choir at her church when we were little. I also remember my entire family, (Mommie, aunts, uncles, brothers, sisters, cousins and granny participating in "Family Day" at Unity Baptist Church. We were the size of a large choir and we have always sung songs together at different churches. We have continued our family legacy of music and at any moment of the day, when we are together, you can hear someone break out in a song!

"Our family tradition and foundation in the word of God has continued to be passed

down from generation to generation, as well as, our legacy of music"

"Family traditions should be passed down from generation to generation so that the family legacy will live on!"

Chapter 5

"School" and the "Big house."

School was always exciting and interesting to me even as a little girl in preschool. I enjoyed coloring and story time tremendously, but my favorite was play time. Oh, how I loved to play in the doll corner. I even got into trouble with Mommie for telling my teacher with strong conviction that I was not taking a nap with the class because I was not done playing in the doll corner. I tried to get out of it by the telling my mom that I did not say no to nap time; I just wasn't ready to stop playing when my teacher called for nap time. Well that was the wrong answer and I got a whooping and was placed on punishment. I quickly learned to follow the rules, not to mention my oldest brother Lloyd ran errands for the school office. Whenever I did the wrong thing in class, my mom told my teacher to let him know and she would handle it. As I look back, this would be my first resentment.

I remember being in my first-grade classroom with my teacher and class peers as we sat watching the news caster talk about the assassination of Dr. Martin Luther King Jr. My teacher along with the other school staff were all crying. All I could remember was feeling like he was as close as a family member to everyone. One thing I knew for sure was that he was extremely important for everyone to be so sad and upset about his dying. When I got home, I told my mom about everyone being so sad. That's when Mommie explained to me who Dr. Martin Luther King Jr. was and the causes he fought for the equality for all mankind. Dr. Martin Luther King Jr. became extra special to me at an early age, as well as, the late President John F. Kennedy. Their lives became examples for me to model about caring for the well-being of others.

The next school year my mom got remarried to Ralph White and we moved to a new neighborhood. Our family moved into a duplex house with 6 bedrooms on each side and a door in the second-floor hallway that allowed us to go on either side. My mom lived on one side and my aunt Dena lived on the other side with my four cousins Harry,

Milly (named after granny) Kiana and Kyre and my granny. The purpose of our move to this house was for my mom to care for my granny during the night while my aunt worked and for my aunt to care for my granny during the day while my mom worked. Our house was known as the "Big House." We always had our family dinners there for years. No matter what the weather turned out to be, rain or shine, it could hold our entire family that was extremely large and continuing to grow.

Moving meant going to a new elementary school "John F. Lowell." My favorite teachers were Mrs. Freely (second grade), Mrs. Yano, (third grade), and Mrs. Monroe (fifth grade). I began playing the violin in second grade, I became a cheerleader in the third grade and I sang in my first talent show in school in the fifth grade with my childhood friends Carrie and Viola. Our school colors were brown and orange and I was as proud as a peacock to be chosen to be in the school activities on any level. I sang in the school choir, joined the band, attended basketball games as a cheerleader, competed in our school Olympics and always won awards. I remained extremely active throughout my school years and participated in everything I could. My granny saw to it that whatever I needed from instruments to a cheerleading outfit, I got. All I had to do was obey my mom rules and get good grades to keep getting privileges. My granny was big on reminding me that I was a lady, as well as, a Christian. She said never curse, slurp, and girls sat with their legs closed or crossed. She also said that the women took care of the inside of the house and the men took care of the outside. Her motto was cleanliness is next to Godliness. She was firm in her belief that as a Christian we represented God and he was to be honored in everything we did and said.

Granny would always tell me "Pretty is as pretty does." "Remember this and you will always be beautiful."

In other words, if you dress a pig up, it will still be a pig!

Chapter 6

"My Teen Years"

When did the word "More" become so important to me? When I turned 13, I remember wanting more of everything. From getting better good grades, all the way down to wanting more hair on my head. I began to long for more and for some reason it had to be the best. I am not sure if this is a result of me growing in my faith in God or if I was simply growing up and realizing that there was so much more to life than I had previously experienced. Whatever the reason, I set out on a quest for Gods Best. This became more evident as I began to develop and grow into a woman. I became conscious of my appearance and began to take longer periods of time getting myself ready in the morning. I drove my brothers and sister's crazy because I could stay in the bathroom for hours. I began playing the piano, and the Baby and Bass Baritone in Jr. High School because they did not have band, instead, they had an orchestra. It got so bad that my brothers and sisters complained to my mom about me playing my instruments, but that didn't stop me from practicing every day after school.

My love for music increased and I began singing for hours on end in my bed room. I continued to sing in the church choir and I had my first concert at age thirteen at Unity Baptist Church. I was so excited and I even got to keep the offering. I remember the very next day after the concert going in the corner store and stealing two Hershey chocolate bars. Back in the day, I learned that all shut eyes are not sleep. I also learned quick that just because Mommie was not there, didn't mean she was not going to find out when I did wrong. Besides, Momma raised us to be respectful and have manners. Where did I get the notion that I could take things that did not belong to me? Granny told me that we were sinners, who were prone to make mistakes, and if I confessed my sins, God would forgive me. My Sunday school teacher told me that we all fall short and nobody was perfect, however, we had to try to stop doing wrong once we asked for forgiveness. My Momma told me that I was on punishment until she said different, after she whooped my behind. That was my first experience with negative consequences and making choices that negatively impacted my reputation. You see, it appeared to me that everyone else considered me to be a goody two shoes. For some reason, they had higher expectations for me and encouraged me to set higher expectations for myself. Which is just what I did. I confessed my sins to God and my mom and became determined to put my past mistakes behind me. Stealing was not an option because the price was too high to pay, as a resident at my Momma's house.

"No matter who we are, we all struggle with our sin nature"

The only person on earth who is without sin was JESUS. Even he called on the name of GOD for strength when in his humanness, he got weak. He showed us how to live life victoriously through prayer.

Chapter 7

"Fashion, Make-up, and Hair"

I became conscious of my hair, skin and nails at an early age and my appearance was extremely important to me as I graduated to Jr. High. Lane Jr. High was an all girl's school. I remember my first day of Jr. High school. My older sister made me walk behind her because I wore my pink Easter dress that I thought was "fly" and I had pink bows in my hair. She warned me not to dress like that and said it was not that type of party. , the older girls made fun of me and the other seventh graders. I vowed to never wear my church clothes to school again. I made up in my mind that this was the last day anyone would make fun of my clothing. I set out to become a fashion queen. Besides, what did my older sister know? All she ever wore was jeans and tennis shoes. I began to watch commercials and read magazines to see what the latest fashions were. I even took sewing class and began making my own clothes.

I loved to spend the weekends with my aunt Pam (Mommie's younger sister) and uncle Johnny and their two kids, Ronnie and Leah who were both younger than me. They took me to church with them every Sunday. My aunt Pam was a big reader of books. She kept magazines and books on the living room table. I learned that I could read a book and travel anywhere in the world, without leaving the house. Aunt Pam and uncle Johnny were so precious to me. I loved them and I admired their marriage. In fact, I was going to have a marriage and a family just like theirs when I grew up. Basically, they spoiled me. If I needed things for school, I could count on their support. In fact, they were a big support to everyone in our entire family. My aunt Pam went to Indiana with my Jr. High school drill team for a competition. We were the only Jr. High school in the competition, and under the direction of Ms. Belinda Carter we came in fourth place. Ms. Carter also directed the school choir that I sang in from the seventh through the ninth grade. She was my second music teacher that encouraged me to sing. Mr. Stevens directed the school orchestra and he would always tell me that I had more talent in my pinkie finger, than most people had in their bodies. Math and Science were the subjects that caused me the most challenges. However, I loved English and Social Studies.

Wouldn't you know it my sin nature cropped up again and I took a pair of my friends (Tory Beavers) shoes that she let me wear during school and kept them. My mom and my granny were so angry with me. I got a long talking to by the both of them and then I was placed back on punishment for a long time. When I think back, there was no reason for me to take the shoes. I had shoes and if I needed shoes or anything else someone in my family would have bought them for me. I took the shoes back to school and in embarrassment, instead of giving them back to her; I placed them in the lost and found. Guess what? Someone took them from the lost and found and no one ever saw those shoes again. My life went down a different path from that day forward. I felt like crap! What ever happened, my granny was always there to encourage me to repent of my sins, my Sunday school teacher told me that no one was perfect but Jesus Christ, and my momma whooped me and told me that I was on punishment until she said different. I spent the entire summer watching everyone else enjoy themselves as I watched from a window in the house. That summer I learned the meaning of the old saying "standing on the outside looking in." The only thing I could do was spend time with my granny and go to church. I learned another hard lesson due to my disobedience.

At age fourteen I got my first job singing in a CYSP summer program. I was so excited about being able to work and buy my own school clothes. It was the best summer of my life and next school year, I was going to be as sharp as a tac. I was determined to put my best foot forward and make better choices. I realized that God gave me insight, wisdom and power to make things happen. All I had to do was pray and believe.

"Look out world, here I come"

No longer would I give people the opportunity to talk about me and make me feel less than others. I set out to show the world who LaTanese was and nobody was going to Stop me, but Mommie and GOD.

Chapter 8

"I Began to Experiment"

"Music, Boys, What's that Smell?"

Music was always my thing. Music was my life and It became my best friend. I would sing all day and all night if Mommie let me. I sang in the church choir, every school choir, our family choir, and in numerous singing groups throughout my childhood and teenage years. Since I was a little girl, until this day, music has been the best way I know to express myself. Somebody told me I had a unique sound, but it had to be marketed, whatever that meant. They said I had a sound like Barbara Striesand or Donna Summer sound, but different. Eventually, my music led me to theater. When I participated in theater, I was compared to a young Melba Moore. Who or whatever they thought I was is not important to me. All I wanted to do was sing. In my early church years, I was known for singing "Said I Wasn't Gonna Tell Nobody" by Alex Bradford and "Changed" by Walter and Tramaine Hawkins. I sang "Our Love" by

Natalie Cole in every talent show in the community.

At 15 my music career took off. I began singing with "The Twilights of Joy" (Gospel) and "Sweet a Harmony" (Secular). I began singing and acting full time and that became my career choice. I started getting paid for performing at age 14. I also sang in school vocal competitions. I placed second place for singing "People" sung by Barbara Streisand from the movie "Funny Girl." I remember feeling important. Mommie and granny kept me grounded and gave balance to my life, as I sang throughout the community. My brothers and sisters reminded me that I still had to do chores and basically let me know that I was not all that every day. I was blessed to get a job from age 14-16 with the CYSP program and continued to develop my musical talents. Things got so busy in my life concerning singing, that I often had long talks with my granny. My granny's advice was to never forget that I am a Christian first. Granny said if I couldn't be a Christian, I shouldn't get involved.

Pursuing music got me out of the house and away from my family. I began to focus completely on developing my own talents and skills. That's when it happened. Boys began noticing me. They were interested in things that were important to me. I developed this thing for musicians. If he could sing or play an instrument, in my mind, we were meant to be. However, in the real world, it didn't always turn out like that.

That's when things began to progress in positive and negative ways. I remember getting one of the leading roles at age 15 in the play "Pinocchio Live." I also remember getting the big head and being corrected by the play director that being selfish and self-centered would not work because the world did not revolve around me. That was humbling to say the least. Not to mention, she reminded me that if I wanted to keep the leading role, I had to remain teachable and be willing to work with everybody. That was my year to grow up fast. I experienced this funny smell at a CYSP cast party after one of the plays we did. Someone told me it was marijuana and warned me not to use it. I never forgot the smell of marijuana from that day forward. Anyhow, I couldn't stay long at the party because Mommie wouldn't allow it and that was the last I saw of my "boy" friend until next summer.

Things changed quickly and the next year was totally different. I was fifteen and I met my first love at the summer jobs. He was perfect for me. His name was Danny Wilson, he was 2 years older than me and boy was he handsome. Not to mention, he was a musician. Danny played in a well-known band in the city called the Monet's. He believed in God and his family was big in the church community. Up until this point of my meeting Danny, my granny and I were inseparable. However, I began to spend less time with her. My life quickly changed and my days consisted of Granny, School, Church, Music and Danny. It appeared that Granny did not mind that much, evidence by her continuing to check on me and making sure I had what I needed to participate in activities. I began talking with Danny on the phone after school for hours. Mommie even talked with Danny's mother (Vivian Wilson) and I got permission to eat dinner with them after church. The best part was they lived across town and I didn't know anyone. I could basically do what I wanted if I was respectful. Little did I know that this relationship would forever change my life. In my eyes, this was the beginning of a beautiful life for me.

"You Know The old saying "sometimes you can't see the forest for the trees, I found out is definitely true"

Sometimes we get involved in things that we have no business getting involved in. Listening to Mommie's advice about life, because she has been there and done that, could have prompted me to live a completely different lifestyle.

Chapter 9

"Do not turn your back on A Golden Opportunity"

I remember Joseph Hall High School like it was yesterday. I sang in the choir and joined the drill team. I often heard comments such as "for a dark-skinned girl she's cute." It wasn't until high school that my older sister and I found out that we weren't ugly; rather, my brothers threatened the boys in the neighborhood not to talk to us. However, some of the boys at school didn't know my brothers and they tried to talk to me and my sister. The ones who did know my brothers warned the ones who didn't about our "crazy" brothers and told them not to talk to us.

I was often chosen to sing solos in the school choir. I sang in high school vocal competitions and became an All City choir member. I was also chosen to sing with the Cleveland Orchestra ensemble. I remember choosing between singing and playing an instrument in high school because choir and band class were at the same time. I could not pursue being a member of the marching band because the drill team and band practiced at the same after school. I chose singing in the choir and being a "High Stepper" on the drill team.

The school music teacher (Mr. Williams), who was also the choir director, told me that I had a raw talent to sing. He encouraged me to pursue music as a career and develop my vocal gift. In the eleventh grade, he set up me an audition to be considered for a scholarship to a college for music in New York. Guess what, I blew it. My aunt Pam and uncle John were so angry with me for messing up what they called a "Golden Opportunity." All I could think was, it was my life and I should make the decisions about how I lived. Boy was I wrong. As I look back, I wish I had listened to Mr. Williams because truthfully speaking, I would probably be music or voice teacher at a College or University today. As I reminisce about my decision to take the scholarship, all I could think of was leaving everything that was familiar to me, especially Danny and I chose not to go.

Mommie, granny, and the other adults who cared about me tried to get me to make wise and healthy choices, but I was just too hard headed and wouldn't listen. They did all they could to keep me on the right path, but because of my stubbornness I continued to learn things the hard way. My granny used to tell me all the time "A hard head makes a soft behind." My granny always encouraged me to remain obedient to God, follow his rules and ask for forgiveness when I was wrong. I always believed that God had great things in store for my life, if I worked hard and kept God first. My message to young people is to listen to wise and Godly advice. Read your Bible and keep praying. Follow the directions of your parents, because the Bible says they have the responsibility of taking care of you. Not to mention, they must give an account to God for how they raise you. You must give an account too for the things you do and don't do. Stay on your best behavior. You never know who is watching you that has the resources and connections to help you reach your highest goals and dreams. Just keep in mind as you begin to make choices about your future, that God wants to give you his Best.

"SOME OPPORTUNITIES COME ONCE IN A LIFETIME!" SO, DON'T BLOW IT!

In hind sight, there were years that I prayed that someone would notice me and give me a chance to share my musical ability. I never forgot that decision to say no to what could have placed me in a different arena in life. I could have received my education long time ago.

Chapter 10

"Mommie Don't Know Nothing"

Have you ever heard the old saying "You can lead a horse to the water, but you can't make it drink?" We'll I continued learning the hard way. My mother was doing the best she could to keep me on the right path; however, I began to stray away from her teachings "BIG Time" which inevitably led to bigger trouble. My adolescent years proved to be extremely challenging for me evidenced by my lying to mom so I could hang out with negative peers in the community. I started rebelling to the point that I even snuck out of the house after Mommie went to sleep a couple of times. I eventually got caught and grounded. I continued to make things difficult for myself by being hard headed and not following the rules. One of the things that were drilled into my head by my granny and Mommie was that God would not bless a mess.

My conscious always let me know when I got too far off track. I could always feel when I was going into dangerous territory. I believed that if I continued to pray, attend church and Bible study, l would eventually find whatever it was l was looking for. I never forgot to this day, to repent when I was wrong and ask God for forgiveness. I was taught by my Sunday school teacher (Nina) that repentance was the only way to experience having a peace of mind. I told her I that was repenting so much and I couldn't stop doing wrong; even when I knew it was wrong. That's when she taught me about the "reprobate mind" found in Romans 1:28. This passage of scripture is about people continuing in sin, turning away from Gods commands and laws, and God allowing them to follow their own beliefs about how they should live, even if that path led of destruction.

I learned the hard way that following Gods way and his plan for your life, is the only way to be blessed and live a successful life. When we refuse to follow sound advice, and become unteachable, we stray into unknown territories, that cause us to make negative choices, that ultimately lead to negative consequences. Refusal to follow Mommie's rules set me on a path of sexual promiscuity and the exploration of illegal substances at age 17. These choices had a long-lasting negative impact on my life!

"The choices we make today effect our tomorrows. "Caution" "Choose wisely!"

Chapter 11

"Looking For Love In All The Wrong Places"

I began to tell Mommie lies so she would give permission to visit Danny the on the weekends. Things weren't going the best at home or in school. After turning down my scholarship, my music teacher was utterly upset with disbelief and it appeared that he was no longer willing to put the effort into helping me develop my musical gifts or talents. I totally didn't get that back then; however, today I get it. I was never one to stay in places of rejection long, even if I caused it. My Mommie raised me to never beg anyone to be with me and my granny always taught me to believe a person when the they shared what was on their minds. She said it would keep me safe and tell me what I needed to do concerning all people and all circumstances. She called it having a discerning Spirit.

I began hanging out with people I grew up with in my neighborhood; however, their lives had drastically changed. Some were invested in going to college and some were involved in relationships with their "boyfriends." Some of them had even become pregnant or already had babies. To tell you the truth, I felt like I really didn't belong anywhere. I continued in the church choir and continued to sing with various artists in the community, but things took a turn in my life as l began to get more involved with Danny. Two years had passed and we were still talking on the phone and kissing whenever we got a chance. He was graduating High School and already had plans to go to his prom with his "girl" friend from school. It was not a big deal for me at the time and we continued to date. We began to spend more and more time talking and getting to know one another. Danny ran track and played the trumpet in a well-known band in our city. Mommie even let him visit me at our house occasionally. I really liked visiting with Danny and his family. He lived with his mom (Viola) brother (Jim) and grandma (Margie). They were always kind to me and it was a lot quieter than my house. He even got along with my brothers and sisters. I really liked Danny and we had a lot in common, such as music and church. Danny smoked "weed" but never pushed me to smoke with him. I guess it was because he hung around older people and played in the clubs on the weekends. He was always a gentleman and extremely good looking and he was also going to college. Eventually, he became my hearts throb and we became inseparable. He proved to me that I could trust him and I lost my virginity to Danny. Eventually, I was lying to Danny's mom so I could spend as much time with him as I could. Because of the lies, I began to ruin the relationship with my mother. She completely lost all trust in me. It got extremely difficult for me to be around my family because everyone was pointing their fingers at little Ms. Goody two shoes. That feeling of not belonging cropped up again. Not to mention, the people I thought would understand began to express their lack of faith and trust in me. This only increased my self-doubt. You see, I had big dreams for myself and when I fell, it was hard. In my mind, it was Danny and me against the world. As long as I had Danny there for me, nothing else mattered.

"Codependency is a type of dysfunctional helping relationship where one person supports or enables another person's drug addiction, alcoholism, gambling addiction, poor mental health, immaturity, irresponsibility, or under-achievement"

Never lose yourself to follow someone else's dreams because if you give them everything you have, when they walk away, they might take you with them. You must keep your own dreams alive, no matter what path you choose in life.

Chapter 12

"What Happened? How did I get here?"

Before long I was at Danny's home every day. I would go home in the evening, go to school and go back to Danny's house without my mom's permission. My granny tried to talk to me, and it helped for a minute. My mom continued to come down hard on me and that only made me more and more rebellious. It was my senior year of high school and I even started skipping school to be with Danny. What was I thinking? Everybody told me to go to school but Danny and I did not connect the dots. Pastor Micha and my Sunday school teacher Nina tried to talk to me about the awesome purpose God had created me for. They encouraged me to get back in school, but I felt like I was so far behind that I couldn't catch up in my classes. My aunt Pam and uncle John were so disappointed in me that it hurt to think about it. It was all my fault because I just wouldn't listen. Eventually, I stopped going to school and became a "high school dropout." I was so embarrassed about how my life was turning out.

Danny was still in college during the weekdays and he continued playing in the band on the weekends. My mom would not allow me to come and go as I pleased, so I started spending the night with Danny on a regular basis. I even started attending church with him. I was known as Danny's girlfriend to Danny's family and friends. Danny and I were sleeping around on a regular and one day my monthly menstrual cycle was late. No one could have ever told me that at seventeen years of age, I would be pregnant! I had really made a mess of my life. This was the lowest point of my young adult years. Not to mention, I had a lot of decisions to make fast. First, I needed to tell Danny that I was pregnant. That went well for Danny because he was 19 years old and considered grown. He told me he would get a job after school and encouraged me to move in with him and his mom. He told his mom that I was pregnant and she was sad at first. However, she embraced me and said she would do all she could to help and she did just that. Ms. Wilson promised to be there for me no matter what I needed.

On the other hand, I had to tell my mother. That did not go well at all. My mother was so angry, upset and disappointed in me. She told me that the choices I made to quit school and get pregnant would one day come back to haunt me. Sad to say, mothers are always right. My granny told my mother to make me get an abortion. My mother told my granny that it was my choice if I wanted to keep my baby. My view of my mother changed drastically. I no longer saw her as the enemy, but instead as an ally. I prayed and gave my baby's life back to God to do whatever he wanted to do with my baby throughout my pregnancy.

I moved back home and my mother made sure that I received the prenatal care I needed to care for myself and my baby under the doctor's care. My mother talked with Danny and his mom about the baby. She let them know that she did not approve of the situation; however, she would not abandon me when I needed her most. Mommie reluctantly accepted the fact that she was going to be a grandma. I think this was because I had three older brothers and one older sister. For the first time in a long time, I tried to rebuild my relationship with my mother. I was glad to be home, but things were never the same. The Devils plan is to ruin your relationships in every area of your life. I imagine the enemy being so proud of himself for the mess and dysfunction he caused in my relationship with my family. The Bible says "Honor thy mother and father for a reason. I truly wanted to follow the plans of God for my life, but my sin nature kept getting in the way.

"Never forget my saying as you continue reading this story "SIN separates us from God" "The wrong you do, will catch up with you"

Chapter 13

"If you need help…Ask"

Things never got better at home between Mommie and I. It was different not just because of the pregnancy, but because as with sin for Adam and Eve in the garden of Eden, my eyes were open to a whole new level of responsibility. Little did I know that my actions would have long lasting negative effects. My relationship with my siblings changed and no one appeared to be concerned about what I needed but me in my home. My oldest brother had joined the National guard and was stationed in New York. My second oldest brother was living with my aunt and her children. My third oldest brother had enlisted in the Army. My oldest sister had just graduated high school and was making plans to go to the Army also. My little brother and sister were still in school and my mom was working as a seamstress for a major sewing company in our city. It appeared that everyone was fine, but me.

I remember feeling so bad about the choices I had made that led me to this place. I would leave the house and go to Danny and his mom for support. They always lifted my spirits when I was with them, but then I had to go back home. I remember going to the Old Arcade and looking over the second-floor balcony down to the lower level. I was so depressed about my situation that my mind told me to jump! Just as soon as I thought about it, my mind said do not listen because Jesus loved me and my life was not over. I sat down at one of the tables and I wrote my first song "Where there's a will there's a way to your happiness" in 1979. I took those words and tucked them deep into my heart and they gave me hope. I still had the same problems, but I knew that God would help me find a solution. I prayed to God for an answer. I prayed that God would send me help and he did. I called Danny and he met me down town. We walked and talked about our situation and he came up with the solution that I should move in with him and his mom, brother (Jim) and grandma (Margie). Danny's mom agreed so that the baby and I would be safe and well taken care of. All I had to do was get my mom to go along with our plan.

Nevertheless, Mommie went ballistic when I told her I was going to live with Danny and his mom. My granny was totally against it, and warned my mother not to let me go. My entire family was in shock and disbelief that I was pregnant and moving in with this guy at age seventeen. This time I had really gone and made a mess of things.

"Negative choices breed Negative Consequences" In other words, you reap what you sow"

Chapter 14

"My Daughter and I"

The months passed quickly and before long, everyone could see what I had done. Some family and friends turned away from me because of my pregnancy and yet, others encouraged me to stay positive and try to make good out of a challenging situation. Their support helped me stay focused on moving forward. This was one of the most difficult times in my life up until this point. My mom never gave me her approval of my living with Danny and his mom and she never let me forget it. I attempted attending my home church, but the ridicule, guilt and shame was too much. Besides, I was told not to participate in any choirs or was not allowed to usher until after my baby was born. It made me feel like an outsider and a failure. Eventually the pain became too much to bear and I stopped attending services. However, I did attend his church regardless to the stares l received from people in their congregation. To my surprise, a lot of the older women encouraged me. These women were dear friends of Danny's mom (Mrs. Carlie and Mrs. Mitchell) who lived on their street. Some told me they were praying for me, and others even prayed with me. Although, I knew I was wrong for getting pregnant out of wedlock, these people were willing to support me and I so needed love and a friend in my life. I spent a lot of time by myself because I really didn't have a lot of friends who accepted my condition near Danny's house. This is when I began writing lyrics to songs. As I look back, I want to thank God that the Monets (Danny's band) practiced in Danny's basement. During the day when Danny was at school and his mom was at work, I had access to the keyboard in the basement and God blessed me to put music to the lyrics.

My doctor became a big supporter of mine and I looked forward to attending my appointments.

I told my doctor my story so he could better help me. My doctor was extremely encouraging and told me to remember to try to stay positive, because the baby could feel what I was feeling. I took the best care of myself I possibly could. I was grateful to have Danny's moms support. I Kept my doctor's appointments and followed his orders. Before long, the "Big Day" arrived and I gave birth to a beautiful bouncing baby girl and named her Nina Lane. She was born December 15, 1979. Weighing in at 7lbs 8 ounces. She was beautiful and bald as "Kojak." This is the day that my life changed forever. As I held my daughter in my arms I cried and gave her back to God in prayer. One thing I know for sure is only God can give life and therefore, I was certain that God had a purpose for me and my child.

Two weeks later, I turned 18. I was grown and had grown up responsibilities. Nevertheless, my Nina needed me and I needed her. I encourage young people to pursue their education or career before starting a family. Having a family means providing for them. I was on public assistance and I began thinking about getting a job so I could take care of Nina and myself. I got a job at "The Shrimp Boat" restaurant working evenings, as a server. I found a babysitter in the neighborhood for Nina. Please believe me when I say, it is easier said than done. I stayed in church and joined the choir at Danny's church. I began leading songs and participating in various groups and events that the church gave. Before long, Danny's and my relationship changed drastically. My life began to get busy with the baby and work. Danny started playing and traveling with his band and I started seeing him less and less. I came home from work one day and another woman was in my house, holding my child, and the introduction was out of order. The word hurt is an understatement for the way I felt. Not to mention, one night after work I caught him cheating on me with our babysitter. Nina and I moved out. I hadn't resolved my issues with my mom so, Nina and I went to live with my Aunt Pam and Uncle John and their two children. Since I attended church with them since age eight and spent my weekends with them as a teenager, moving in with them was like old times. This led me back to my home church and I repented of my sins and renewed my membership. I began singing in the choir and attending Sunday School.

I was young mom with a 12month old daughter and a "high school drop out." I had to find another way to make a decent living for myself and my child. I was determined to continue my education and returning to high school was out of question, so I enrolled in GED classes. After a while, I moved back home with my mom and brothers and sisters. After you leave home and go back as an adult, things will never be the same. I remember the day I got my GED in the mail. I was so excited because the test was hard and I was not sure if I scored high enough to pass. I shared the news with my family and they appeared not to care, evidenced by one of my brothers congratulating me, and asked "What was for dinner and if I was the one cooking?"

"If you fail to deal with your issues in life, you just carry it with you wherever you go"

"If children do not resolve their childhood issues, they just carry them into Adulthood"

"I was still trying to define who I was as a young woman and I had no clue about how to be a mother"

Chapter 15

"Beauty School and Music"

I never forgot the message that God wanted his best for me. All I needed to do was have faith and believe in God and take him at his word. I began to explore ways to better my life and my income. Not to mention, welfare only lasted so long every month and my daughter's father did not pay child support. I always try to discourage young people from becoming young parents because it is hard enough taking care of yourself, let alone providing for a child. Some people make it look easy, while others experience great difficulty and hardship being a parent. It's twice as hard without the support of the child's other parent. I believe that is one of the bigger reasons God forbids us not to have sex until after marriage. Raising children is a big responsibility and commitment that must not be taken lightly.

I was faced with many questions after my break up with Danny. How was I going to provide for Nina and I?

Where would we live? These top two questions proved to be definite reoccurring issues in my life. It wasn't easy, but after a lot of thought and prayer, I enrolled in "Vogue Beauty School" to become a licensed cosmetologist and to top it all off, Nina and I moved into our own apartment. It was only 3 rooms, but it was enough for Nina and I. My granny's words and teachings came back to my mind over, and over again, as I began this new chapter in my life. One saying was "I didn't live this long by being stupid" and the other saying was "Always remember that the Lord will make away somehow." I became more and more determined to make a life for Nina and myself.

I began following my dreams to sing again. I continued to sing in church and even sang in talent shows in the community. I won numerous talent shows all over the city. Eventually, I graduated beauty school. My oldest sister agreed to go to the state board in Columbus, Ohio, as my model and I became a licensed cosmetologist in March 20, 1984. My first job was a nail technician at Leroy and Company Barber Salon. It didn't pay a lot, so I began working for my family's hair salon that was thriving. The Jerri Curl was huge and they came out with their own product that swept the city. I was making money and was finally able to live comfortably. Things went so well that I was able to buy a car for Nina and I. I would drop Nina off at her grandmothers so I could work. I began partying after work on the weekends. After a while of working in the salon, my body began to get sick from breathing in the chemicals per the doctor's report. His statement was devastating as he told me I would either sing or do hair because I couldn't do both breathing in the hair chemicals. I made the decision to stop working at the salon because of my love for music. God had given me the gift of music before I had anything else and I wasn't about to lose my voice just to make money. Besides, my granny assured me that God still had a plan for my life and she encouraged me to pray and seek God for an answer. No job meant signing back up for public assistance so Nina and I could keep our apartment, pay bills, and eat. Besides depending on another person for help at this time was out of the question.

That's when it happened. I heard about an audition for gospel singers for the play "Tambourines to Glory" at Karamu House Theater. I prayed over and went to the audition. I got the part as "Marietta." I was so happy to be back to doing what I loved to do. It was an awesome experience. I reconnected with some friends from the plays I was in as a teenager and made new acquaintances in the world of theater. I didn't get paid for performing but that was okay with me because I was on public assistance. It was worth the sacrifice to me because all I ever wanted to do was sing. I was still a member at Danny's church and the church bought bulk tickets to see the play. After "Tambourines to Glory" ended I auditioned for another play, "HMS Pinafore." I got the understudy role as "Josephine" the captain's daughter. I was nominated as best new performer for the "84-85" season. In my excitement, I shared the news with my family. My granny encouraged me that God would bless my work and to remain faithful. She and I prayed for Gods will to be done in my life. Guess what? I won "Best New Performer" for the 1984-1985 Season at Karamu House. Truth be made known, there were times I wanted to give up at Karamu because of people and their fickle ways. I tried to open-up and befriend some people who had not befriended me and got hurt after forming some unhealthy relationships. I was feeling down one day and a tall light skinned kind gentleman, carrying a guitar approached me in the halls at Karamu and asked me was I okay. I don't know why I told him my business, but I told him that I was discouraged and wanted to leave Karamu House. He encouraged me and said, "Whatever you do, don't quit your singing; you have something special that you can share with people all over this world." I never forgot that and I'm glad I persevered because my next stop was Hawaii for five weeks of recording music and fun in the sun.

"I am a living witness that God will send you what you need, right when you need it"

Chapter 16

"New Opportunities and New Adventures"

My childhood friend Kyle Micha, whose parents were my pastor and First Lady at Unity Baptist church, heard some of my music. He liked it so much that he invited me to come to Hawaii to record with himself and members of the Marine Corps Band. It was such an honor and I am glad I said yes. The invite couldn't have come at a more perfect time. I was struggling to pay my rent and bills and most of the time Nina was with Danny's mom because she hadn't started school yet. I told her about my plans to record with Kyle and asked her to watch Nina for me while I went to Hawaii and she agreed. We moved from our apartment and settled Nina in with her grandmother and I made plans to travel. It was my first time flying and it took 12 hours and two time-changes to get there. When we touched ground, I got on my knees and prayed. It was one of the most beautiful places I have ever seen in my life and I will never forget being there.

I stayed in Waipahu, Hawaii in the mountains. I stayed with friends of Kyle who were married. They had a beautiful apartment off the beach. I had my own room with a view of the beach that was breathtaking. That night I called Nina and every night after that until I returned home. I missed and loved her so much. Kyle lived on the Marine base and picked me up every day after work for practice. I am grateful for the opportunity to travel and experience other cultures throughout the world. During the day, I exercised, wrote songs, read books, and relaxed by the pool. I met wonderful people who embraced me and my talents and gift of music. One day while sitting by the pool, I met an older Caucasian gentleman who inquired about my being in Hawaii. I informed him that I was there to record and he laughed. I was thinking to myself to steer clear because he had a few lose screws. He then proceeded to tell me his wife was a musician who played for one of the elite hotels as entertainment. He set a time for me to join them for dinner so I could meet her. He was a retired businessman and she was a retired music teacher. I told them my story and about my love for music. She played the piano and I sang for her. She told me I had "raw" talent and assured me that it was a good thing to have because I could develop it through training. I was grateful to meet them because I made new friends in Hawaii.

I also met another young couple who were both in the military. I hung out with them when Kyle was busy doing military things. Kyle met them and agreed that it would be okay for me to get out of the house and sight see sometimes. I got into some trouble while waiting for Kyle one day after sneaking into the marine's barracks. Kyle told me to wait for him inside the barracks because he got off early and we were going to go to Honolulu. Well, I didn't listen and went out to buy a pop from the pop machine. I got caught by a Sargent trying to re-enter the barracks. I was horrified. He called me a

"*Civilian*" and ordered me to wait outside. I got scolded and checked and never went to the barracks again.

I am thankful to my friend for allowing me the opportunity to travel to such a beautiful place. The only thing I regret is not taking Nina with me. Kyle told me that should have brought her with me so I could have stayed longer. As the old saying goes, Hawaii is a beautiful place to visit, but I wouldn't want to live there. After the recording was completed, I returned home and resumed life as a single mom and continued seeking away to provide for Nina and myself.

"Sometimes we get golden opportunities to see what life is like on the other side. If we are not ready, we miss the bigger picture of what God is saying. Here's to whoever said, "Sometimes we have to stop and smell the roses"

Chapter 17

"Trying to find my "Fit" in life!"

Nina was getting so big and it was time for her to begin school! Kindergarten was an exciting time in her life! My little girl was growing up. We moved back in with Danny's mom. However, things were never the same between Danny and I. I was always blessed to have Danny's moms support and God knows I needed it. Danny continued to play the field and I stayed focused on finding a Job. Danny became involved in the club life with his band and began using drugs. I hung out with him and the band members one night and experimented with marijuana and freebasing cocaine. Everything about that scene was wrong. It opened me up to another dimension in life. I experienced a high that I could not explain and I must admit it was a scary ride. After that night, I prayed and I made a promise to myself to never freebase again.

I pulled my cosmetology license out and got busy looking for a job. Being a licensed cosmetologist afforded me the opportunity to do hair, skin and nails. I prayed and got a new job at "Glemby's" hair salon as an aesthetician in May Company downtown Cleveland. I was hired to promote a skin care line of products and do facials and body waxing. The catch to the job was that I had to hustle. If I didn't sell products and do services, there would be no paycheck. I was also trained in aesthetics and things began to take off for me. I prayed and got an apartment for Nina and I. Nina continued to stay with her grandma during the week to attend school, so I could work. I would go to see Nina every day after work and we spent the weekends together. She was my life. Nothing gave me greater joy than being able to provide for Nina and myself. I was determined to make things work for me and they did until I got laid off due to the company downsizing. I was offered to go out to "Beachwood Mall" to work; however, transportation was an issue. It was a big "oh no" and "here we go again." We had to move from our apartment.

I prayed and asked my mom if Nina and I could move back home. This was a humbling time in my life. For the first time, I began to appreciate my momma in a whole new light. When I think about it, she has been there for me the whole time. We settled in and I began looking for a job and Nina attended my old elementary school. I even got the leading role in a play called "Until the Vinegar Runs Out." That's when I met my best friend Angela Simpson. She was older than me, but she was always trying to help me make things better for myself and Nina. She was my angel in the flesh and God knows that I needed and appreciated her in my life. I continued to job hunt and eventually, I got hired as a cashier at Sohio gas station. I was always a hard worker and quick study. I was always taught to give my best in everything I do. Soon, I had the reputation of being dependable and trustworthy. That's when "IT" happened. I met "Steven Tiggs Jr. Little did I know that life was taking me to another level.

"Our Own desires can sometimes trap us into a lifestyle of deception and pain"

"Pray over the small and big decisions you make in your life and always keep God first"

Chapter 18

"My First Marriage"

I was a floater at Sohio, which means I had to cover shifts at gas stations throughout the community. I worked for a total of three service stations until I got hired for a permanent day time position. Hard work will definitely pay off. For another moment in time, my life is back on track. I was so grateful to be able to pay bills and provide for Nina and I. Just when things were going well, Mommie and I were beginning to be at odds again with the home situation. I guess she had a problem with how I was living my life and raising my daughter. It came down to me choosing to follow her rules or finding another place to stay. I was used to being on my own and I missed having my own space. Mommie and I had another "big" falling out, so Nina and I had to move once again. A childhood friend of mine (Cloe), who knew I was having problems with Mommie, asked if I wanted to rent her third-floor apartment. It was perfect for us and I could afford it. She had a son and her nieces and nephews lived next door to her. Nina had someone to play with, not to mention it was right around the corner from Mommie's house. Nina did not have to change schools and the bus line dropped us off right in front of our church for services.

This is when I began to experience the faithfulness of God and I began to know him as provider. I kept getting myself into these "jackpots" and God kept getting me out. I learned to never underestimate the power of prayer in any situation I faced. There is something to be said about having a space that affords you a "p*eace*" of mind. I also began to learn about tranquil moments that are created from being in a good space. My weekends were my time to rejuvenate and relax. Nina and I began spending lots of time together except when her grandmother (Vivian) wanted to see her. The guy who worked the service station with me on days was named Stephen Tiggs Jr. Little did I know that he had been paying close attention to me. I thought he was cool and somewhat attractive so when he asked me to go out with him, I said "yes." Let me just say this before I forget, I learned the hard way "To never mix business with pleasure. We seemed to have a lot in common such as dancing, music and first and foremost, going to church. He had two children, Simone 3 years old and James 2 years old. I told him about Nina who was 5 years old. His dad was a deacon at their church and his mom was one of the sweetest ladies I ever met. Although, Stephen couldn't carry a note in a bucket, his love for God made him perfect for me.

We began to spend lots of time together on the weekends, not to mention all the time we spent on the job. I even attended his church and met his parents (Stephen Tiggs Sr. and Adaline Tiggs). They welcomed me and Nina into their home and the rest is history. Stephen and I smoked marijuana and drank alcohol together. That's when I noticed a different side to Steven. He hit me! It was physical and mental abuse, evidence by him putting his hands on me and promising never to do "it" again. He had a problem for hitting me and I had a problem for staying after he hit me. I wanted to believe and trust him so bad, so I forgave him and we began our love story again.

"Let me pause here to say that when physical abuse begins, it is a strong indicator that the person causing the harm has a serious problem. This type of behavior must be addressed or it will continue throughout the relationship"

I got pregnant after a year of dating Stephen and we decided to get married. When I found out I was pregnant, I prayed and gave my baby's life back to God to use anyway he wanted. Let me encourage anyone who is considering marriage to pray, pray and pray again before taking this step. Stephen was a great provider. He made sure that Nina and I had a roof over our heads, food to eat and transportation. I thought I had arrived. Nina and I moved in with Stephen. The only drawback was that Nina had to change schools. She appeared to adjust well, or so I thought.

(Today, I believe that parents should ask their children how they feel about making major decisions. I believe that some family changes should involve communication, especially when children are involved)

Stephen and I got married on May the 21, 1988. It was a beautiful wedding with a wedding party of 15 people. Nina and Simone were the flower girls and James was the ring bearer. Our colors were cream and royal blue. My mother made my wedding dress, as well as, all the bridesmaids and flower girls. Family and friends showed up for the big occasion and showered us with so much love. I committed to God first, that I would honor him and be a faithful wife to Stephen. On our wedding day, I completely gave Stephen my heart and soul.

(There is something to be said about giving a person your soul, because If they are not as committed as you are, they can almost cause you "irrevocable" pain).

We had a beautiful family and we were expecting our first child together. We moved into a nicer neighborhood and Nina changed schools for the fourth time. I never thought about the impact this was having on Nina. As usual, it appeared to me that Nina adjusted well to having a new step-father. On August 9, 1988, Stephenie Nita was born. Weighing in at 8lbs and 1 ounce. Our daughter was absolutely gorgeous and she looked just like Stephen. I prayed that God would keep his loving arms of protection around her and that she would grow to be and receive everything in her life God had planned for her.

I remember the day things changed like it was yesterday. I was sharing something that was extremely important to me with Stephen and he simply shrugged his shoulders and said, "Oh Well." I asked if he heard me and repeated myself. He then turned to me and said, "I don't care and that's not my problem." I was 100 percent devastated. I retreated to our bedroom, without a word. I sat there in the dark with tears streaming down my face. Thank God that Stephenie was sleeping. I began to feel that horrible pain again like I did when he hit me for the first time when we were dating. Only this time, the blow left no scare, instead, only a wound deep in my soul. Sad to say, I became acquainted with verbal and emotional abuse. The darkness within him continued to grow; only I couldn't see it and did not know when it would rear its ugly head. We continued to stay involved in church and connected with our families. However, I never shared what I was going through with any of them. Today, I know that it was only the power of God that kept me and my children safe.

On several occasions, Stephen would hit me, beg for my forgiveness, and then he would buy me a car or a living room set, or something else extravagant to make me forget the pain. Immediately, I knew it was wrong. Yet, I stayed to hide the hurt, shame, and abuse of a marriage gone wrong. Why didn't I leave? Why couldn't I walk away? What was wrong with me? I was so embarrassed about the beatings that I hid it from family and friends. Stephen tried to seclude me from everyone. However, some of my family and friends are diehards. They knew something was wrong, because they knew me. He would threaten to do harmful things to the people I loved, so I never said a word to anyone. He began to physically and verbally abuse me with an intent to cause me harm. Eventually, I got close to his sister (Bianca) and she shared with me that this was learned behavior. Her report was that since I came into the family, their father had changed. I never witnessed anything but loving behavior from my father in law. As I look back, I honestly believe his abuse was intentional so he could have some form of control over me. As demented as that is, I believe it was the only way he knew to rule over me. Oh, before I forget, I never stopped singing. I remained in the choir and sang at weddings, funerals and talent shows. Whenever I talked about singing, Stephen would allow me to sing in a talent show! I believe he thought that this would suffice my desire to sing. (Really)

Never let anything or anyone strip you away from those things that God has called you to. These things are your destiny and it is where God wants you to be. Stay determined to fulfill your call and communicate the importance of these activities in your life.

Just a hint: "Otherwise, you will remain restless and unfulfilled"

"Living life with no purpose is pointless and a waste of precious time"

Chapter 19

"Love has Everything to do with it!"

I stayed through the good and the bad times of our marriage as suggested by Pastor Micha on the day of my marriage. After all,

Pastor Micha always had my best interest in mind, and besides, Stephen was my husband and I still loved him. However, things were changing drastically for the worst, and so was I. Honestly speaking, I never was the same after he hit me. It was as if something inside of me snapped and broke. I couldn't put my finger on exactly what happened, but I knew, I would never be the same. Could anyone else see my pain? I tried to look prettier, I got a dozen new hairstyles, I tried to cook more interesting meals, and I kept the house spotless and made sure the kids were well kept. Nothing I did ever seemed good enough! Why wasn't I comfortable in my own home?

I can remember Stephen drinking Canadian Mist or Windsor liquor on Holidays and the weekend. As usual, everything went to HELL! It never failed that every time he began to drink, disaster would follow. One thing I will say though is that he never let anyone see him hit me. Stephen was smart because if no one knew what he was doing to me, there would always be the question of it was true or not. I began to die internally, within my own self. My hopes, my dreams, my goals, my future became trapped inside of me and for the first time I felt lifeless inside. I ran into one of my cousins Alita, whom I hadn't seen for years and she looked at me and said, "What happened to you?" Where is your glow? Marriage is supposed to make you shine! Her words haunted me. I laughed and shrugged it off, but she knew me. I needed to tell someone, but it wasn't time. I was determined to fight for my marriage and I tried everything I could think of and nothing seemed to work.

What is fidelity in a marriage? Can you believe that we lost our commitment to be true to one another? Stephen had a girlfriend and it tore me up inside. He began the physical and verbal abuse on a regular. After feeling unloved, abandoned and alone, I moved out. I met this guy who told me I was beautiful; one thing led to another and the rest is history. Sometimes, when you are not getting what you need at home, you look for things elsewhere. We begin to think that the grass is greener on the other side. This is a "huge" trick of the enemy. (If you would water your own grass it would be green too." Once you take a walk on the wild side in your marriage, you and the marriage will never be the same). Today I can say that there is no reason to break my commitment to God, in my marriage. I believe that you cause your own internal destruction by allowing outside influences to destroy your home, family, marriage, and life in general. Was it worth it? Definitely Not! In a marriage, when you love, love hard. When you give, give everything. If you need advice, talk to someone who has years of marriage experience that can validate their information. My aunt Paula would always say, "I am not going to let anyone else reap the benefits of what I have worked hard to build." With these words in mind, we got back together and tried to give our marriage another chance. This time, we moved out of town, but sadly to say, things were never the same.

"There is no Geographical cure. You must address the root cause or when you move the problem moves with you"

Chapter 20

"College Park, Georgia"

We moved to the incredible city College Park, in the state of Georgia in August of 1991. I felt like things were going full circle because my granny was born in Athens, Georgia. Somehow our move represented a second chance. This time I was going to do things completely different. I had recommitted myself to my marriage and was determined that nothing was going to stop us from starting all over again. College Park was breathtaking! This is a city where African Americans can rebuild, grow and be successful. We had recommitted our lives to one another and it even appeared that we had fallen in love again. Stephen had family and friends in Georgia. At first, they made me feel welcome. They had cook outs and Sunday dinners on the weekends. His uncle Greg told me that they drank beer and made babies in Georgia. It felt good to have something to look forward to again, besides, I wanted my family, and I wanted my husband.

Finally, I felt like living again. I settled in, enrolled Nina in School and found an adequate daycare for Stephenie. Since, I transferred my job location to College Park; I was expected to be at work in two weeks.

We pulled my car down on the back of our U-Haul so the girls and I could get around. Boy, did I miss home. We lived in a beautiful apartment with a beautiful view. At the time, Stephen was working in construction. He was second to none when it came to provision for his family. The girls and I were always taken excellent care of. I found a church home not far from where we lived. Things appeared to be going good. And then it happened. Stephen got drunk and hit me, only this time there was no apology. To top it all off, I also noticed a vaginal discharge and questioned him about it. He only replied that I should go and see the doctor. I had contracted a sexually transmitted disease from my husband. Tricked and betrayed again, only this time, I was stuck in Georgia. This set me back into the poor me syndrome. I was filled with regret for leaving home. I felt completely hurt, abused, and alone. However, I had to keep it together for the girls. I learned how to smile through tear stained eyes. I learned how to walk and hold my head high, when inside I was falling apart. I even learned how to dress up real pretty on the outside, when all the while; I was slowly dying on the inside. There I was again, up at night, while everyone was asleep, crying and wondering to myself, how did I let this happen again. My only peace was my relationship with God. I prayed and stayed and once again tried to live up to my marriage vows.

I had to do something to improve life for the girls and I, so I enrolled in to Travel and Tourism School. I completed the course and graduated with honors. I really tried to make Stephen proud of me, But the abuse continued. Nothing ever seemed to be good enough for him. He even belittled me in front of his family. One night he told me that I was replaceable. Life for me was never the same for me in Georgia. He had isolated me from everybody who loved me and it cost a lot to phone home. Not to mention, I was too embarrassed to tell a soul that things between Stephen and I were a mess again. On top of all that, I was pregnant. I knew that the trust I had in my husband was gone, and I really did not care to stay in Georgia. But, I was determined to have my baby. I knew it was a boy. He was my son, and I called him my teacher because his birth made me strong enough to leave. I began packing until the day I left. He knew I was leaving, so I got rid of everything little by little. I rented a U-Haul and the girls and I left to return home.

"We only get one life to live. To thine own self be true"

"If you are unhappy why should you stay in a relationship and be miserable and have those emotions spill into the lives of your children and those who love you"

Chapter 21

"Returning to Cleveland, Ohio"

I tried to pick up the pieces and start again. I moved with a friend when I first came back from Georgia and eventually, ended back at Mommie's house! Sometimes it gets worse before it gets better! My Mother is amazing and finally I could see what she had been telling me the whole time. Make sacrifices for your children because you only have them for a little while and then they become grown and move out. I began to focus on the girls and myself. I got back in the church and started singing with a new Gospel group. Things were going well again. The baby was growing and my stomach was getting huge. My youngest brother (Landon) lived with Mommie too. He was great with the girls and was an excellent cook. When I "say" we ate good, I mean the cooking was excellent. He had a great sense of humor and he kept us laughing and in tears. I saved lots of money and bought things that the baby would need. I was finally healing emotionally from my broken marriage and that's when it happened. Stephen called and said come home.

I don't know what I was thinking. Maybe it was the fact that I grew up without my dad that made me return home. Maybe it was the fact that I wanted my kids to be raised by their father. Well, whatever the reason, I considered Stephens request and began making plans to return to Georgia. I gave birth to my incredible son Stephen Tiggs III on July 20, 1993. He was adorable. 8lbs and 3oz and he looked just like his Stephen and his father. The bond between a mother and son is so beautiful. We lived with Mommie and once again she was my major help and supporter. I talked with her about returning to Georgia and she encouraged me to try to work things out with my husband. Nina, Stephenie, Stephen III and I moved back to Georgia once again, to try to live as a family with Steven. After all, our vows said, for better or worse, for richer or poorer, till death do us part. I prayed and thought I heard GOD say Go Back? Before school started back Stephen was moving Nina, Stephenie, Stephen, and I back to Georgia. The sad part is, I never once discussed it with the kids, nor did I stop to think about how it affected them emotionally. If I was going through, what were they experiencing going back and forth?

"Make sure it's God, before you make your Move"

"Sometimes we act on our own desires without praying, meditating and listening to God"

Chapter 22

"Living A Lie"

We moved into another apartment complex that bigger and better. For me it represented a fresh start for Stephen, Nina, Stephenie, Stephen III and I. By now Nina was in Middle school and Stephenie was in Kindergarten. I found a great daycare for Stephen III and I set out to look for a job. I was determined to keep my marriage together this time. I was so happy. I truly loved my husband and remember, I grew up without my father and I did not want the children to experience that same feeling of wondering why their father never called or came to see them. I got a new job working as a security officer at Delta Airlines Executive Offices. I went to classes for training and got a certificate. At first, I worked nights because that was the only shift they had, however, it was not long before I went to days. I worked the security check point. I would get compliments on my behavior by the employees who entered and exited the facilities. I was at the security station one morning and to my surprise, my supervisor asked me to work as a receptionist on Fridays. I was flabbergasted. My life was taking an upwards turn and I felt like could continue to grow as an employee at Delta Airlines. I even met the president of Delta "Rollen Author." One morning a pilot came in, looked at me, threw his bags down, lifted his hands and said, finally, somebody with style. He made my day! I felt good about myself again. I met a lot of people from various walks of life. I met women who worked at Delta Airlines during the day and were either students at night or strippers in the night club. I was told it was how they made their lives better or so they could make ends meet to take care of their children. Nevertheless, I was told by everyone I met that Georgia is a place where African Americans can thrive and grow. The sky was the limit. Not to mention Georgia is a beautiful place and the weather is awesome.

I joined church and I was asked to sing on a couple of programs. The best part was Stephenie got baptized at age 5. Nina made new friends and reunited with her former friends. I was so happy for her. But something still was not right. I couldn't put my finger on it, but Stephen was different. Stephen never came to church with us. In fact, I was getting the kids ready for church and asked if he was coming. He said no, I am going to stay home and drink. Shortly after that, it happened again. He got drunk and he hit me. I thought I was hiding it from people. All I could do was pray. The pain inside became too much to bear and started drinking Stephens liquor. It worked to help me relax and forget the pain of my husband's verbal abuse, the hurt of my husband hitting me, and the shame of moving back with Stephen, only to realize that he would probably never change his abusive ways, not even for me!

I remember meeting him and his friends at a night club on his birthday after work. I went end to look for him and saw him on the dance floor with a girl getting it on! Hurt is an understatement. I saw some of her friends trying to warn her that I was there, but neither one of them noticed me and continued to be all over one another. When Stephen looked up and saw me, he let her go and grabbed me to the dance floor. Stephen was lit! Now it appeared that everyone was watching the show. I jerked away from him and left the club and went home! As I drove home I became numb inside. I had seen it all! What was I going to do? All I knew was I had to do something. When Stephen got home that night he was so drunk, that he went straight to bed. Thank God, he did because I was not in the mood and besides, the kids were asleep. That night I came up with the bright idea, to get my own place. I was tired of moving back to Cleveland and uprooting my children, so I resolved to find us a place of our own. I had a job and I was going to make it work, without him knowing it. A new nightmare had begun in my life. Once again, I had to deal with his women too!

I questioned him the next morning about his behavior and he told me that he did not remember anything that he had done. I told him to ask his friends to see if I was lying. He asked them and told him of the things he had said and done. This was my first understanding of what it means to be in a "blackout." A person is fully awake; however, they are unable to remember things. The pain inside began to grow and grow and instead of praying and staying involved in the church, I began drinking alcohol because Stephen always had some in the house. The alcohol was not enough so I began to seek other ways to numb my pain. There was a girl at Delta Airlines that smoked marijuana, who told me about club in Atlanta, where you could get any drug you wanted. Unknowingly, I had been set me up for an outlet if I needed one to purchase drugs.

I was not in a good place mentally, so I called my mother and my bestie and told the about what was happening. Mommie encouraged me to work it out and Angela told me if I needed her she would do whatever she could to help me and the kids. I told her of my plans to get a car and move into my own place. She said, I might have to come home. My head was so messed up one day from hurt and shame that I went down to the club and bought me some marijuana and cocaine and began to lace joints. Little did I know that this was the beginning of a very dangerous relationship between me, alcohol, marijuana, and cocaine. Eventually, I saved money and brought me a brand-new car. I tried hard to take care of the kids and continue to work.

One day Stephen went from hitting me behind closed doors to hitting me in front of the kids. He threatened to harm me on two occasions and I called the police both times. I'd never called the police on him before and he was furious. The last time I called the police the officer encouraged me to leave Stephen. Instead, I stayed and worked and struggled with taking care of the kids. I still had plans to move into my own place so I could get away from Stephen. I was unknowingly becoming addicted to alcohol and drugs. The worst part is that the more drugs I used, the more I moved away from my goal to get my own place. I thought about moving back home, but I needed a plan in place. Stephen even approached me when he noticed me packing some boxes. After all, I had left him before, so he knew the signs. I absolutely hated him for how he treated me. I felt one hundred percent used and abused. Why did I have to take this abuse? How dare he judge me when he was an alcoholic and a functioning alcoholic at that. We had everything in home. TV's in every room. I had the best of anything a wife could ask for material wise, which means I had everything except Stephens love. My attitude changed drastically towards him. When he touched me, it literally made me sick to my stomach. I knew the marriage was at its end besides; I was using alcohol and drugs to forget the pain.

I remember being on a constant run to destruction! Day in and day out my thoughts were about running away from Stephen. Running away from myself and the hurt that I could not stop feeling inside of me. I begin to use alcohol and drugs endlessly and the end results were never satisfying. I was losing myself and my mind. Stephen told me that if I was in Georgia I was his. I told Stephen that the kids and I were moving back home and Mommie was expecting us. I got smart about it so that he would know people knew what was going on to prevent him from trying anything crazy. I was bankrupt emotionally and spiritually bankrupt. Stephen had told me so many times that nobody wanted me and I started believing him. That's when I decided enough was enough and moved back to Cleveland. My life was never the same after that. Every day was a day filled with emptiness and shame. Mommie let us move in, but my use continued once I moved home to Cleveland. My father in law died and Stephen moved back to Cleveland to help his mother, and guess what? He brought his girlfriend and her three kids to Cleveland with him. It took everything I had to stay sane. I tried to go back to church and get a job, but my addiction alcohol and drugs had taken place in my life. Eventually, I lost my car and Mommie told Stephen to come and get the kids and they moved in with Stephen and his new family.

The lesson for me in this is remembering that a goal can be set, even it leads to nowhere. The truth is to stay focused so that nothing deters you from your destination! You must stay focused and work hard to accomplish things be it great or small! I also learned a lot about not wasting my time!

"Trust me when I say, "Get Yours!" Everybody else is getting theirs, so you should too"

"Always ask yourself is this what I want or what God wants for me?"

Chapter 23

"East Cleveland"

I felt like Olivia in the song that the "Whispers" sang about because I felt lost and turned out!!! My world had come to a complete stop. Numb inside is an understatement. I lived at home with Mommie until I got a place of my own. Mommie thought the break from the kids would help me get back on track. She encouraged me to go back to church and get a job. I was successful and got the kids back after moving to in my own place in East Cleveland, Ohio. Now, a single mother on

Public Assistance, no transportation and struggling to live and stay sane after my crashing fall!!! Once again, the question hit me but this time it knocked me down.
"HOW DID I GET HERE?"

Nina was living with her grandma and Stephenie, Stephen III and I were together. This was one of the worst places in I ever imagined myself as a married woman. The continuous abuse from my marriage had robbed me of everything good except my children. I was struggling with an "Addiction" that I didn't know I had. The Devil had set me up and I did not know what I was getting myself into in East Cleveland. You see in East Cleveland drugs, sex, and crimes ran ramped. It was the perfect place for my addiction to grow and mature and continued to cause my demise. I knew nothing about the streets but I learned quickly how to survive in a world of darkness. I met a drug dealer and the rest is history. I stopped paying my bills and taking care of the children. I isolated from my family and whenever I went around them it was a horrible experience. We argued or fought all the time. I knew that I was messed up and I really did not need another put downs so I stayed away from them. It got so bad that I would leave the children home for hours by themselves as I ran after and chased down my next high.

Crack Cocaine had become my very best friend and five minutes without it was too much. You see, whenever I got high, I forgot about my failed marriage and the hell and abuse I faced day after day at the hands of the one who was supposed to love and cherish me. I forgot about not being a good mother to my children. I forgot about my family taunting me and laughing about the mistakes I made in my life. I forgot about not fulfilling my dreams to become somebody great and wonderful in my life. I wanted to forget and Crack Cocaine allowed me to forget. Whenever I smoked Crack I forgot all my worries, cares, concerns, and past and present failures. I began a serious relationship with Crack and I completely and totally fell in Love. Crack was my master and I moved at its command. I did whatever my new lover told me to do. I had just about sold everything I had. I was at an even lower part in my life and God still sent me a miracle.

I remember the day I got a call from my Aunt Mimi who said she had found my daddy and gave me his phone number. I was in shock. How could this be? God answered a prayer of mine when I was at my worst. I needed some help because I did not know what had happened to my life. I did not know what was wrong with me. I called him and he came to meet me and Stephen III. By now, Stephenie had gone to live with her father and only came to spend time with me on the weekends. God knows I was struggling and any help was appreciated. Daddy came by and it was everything I could hope for he apologized for not being in my life when I was growing up. I told him that I was going through a divorce and could understand what might have happened between Mommie and him. I caught him up with my past accomplishments. I even sang for him and he loved it. I showed him pictures of my brothers and sisters and Nina and Stephenie. He told me that I had two more brothers and two more sisters that did not know about us. To me that meant that I could not come to daddy's house. That was okay with me because God had blessed me with my daddy and I ran it in the ground. Daddy, daddy, daddy.

I told Mommie and my brothers and sisters about daddy. I even took daddy by Mommie's house to see her. My oldest sister Laurene was there and she met daddy and got his number. Mommie and daddy went into the house to talk and when he came out he was different. My daddy drove me back to East Cleveland and we talked about what Mommie had shared with him about me. I was so embarrassed, but it was the truth. I was addicted to alcohol and drugs and I needed help, but only I did not know I needed help. I lied to daddy to get money and I guess his guilt made him give me money. That lasted for a little while until he said no, but that didn't stop me from getting what I needed. My addiction was now full blown.

Stephenie came over to visit one weekend and it started off great that Friday night. We watched movies and ate popcorn like old times. Nina was 16, Stephenie was seven and Stephen III was two years old. I got my check the next day and everything went straight to hell. I remember leaving the house for hours that day to go get high. I brought Stephenie and Stephen a bag full of junk. Candy, chips, and pop. I remember walking away and looking at them in the window. But little did I know that a concerned neighbor had been watching me leave my children in the house by themselves all day. The last time I left to go get high and came back home, my children were gone. When I opened the door, there was complete and total silence. Where were my children? There was no forced entry so someone must have let them in. I picked up the phone and there was a stutter which meant a message was waiting. I called the message center and it was Nina. She said not to worry because Stephenie and Stephen were safe. She said that the police had called my Mommie and Aunt Pam came to get Stephenie and Stephen and told me call them. I cried and felt pain like never before. My heart ached and I began to sob uncontrollably. And then it happened. I snapped out of it. Instead of me calling to check on my children, I had another brilliant ideal. No kids meant no responsibility, which meant that I could get high all day and all night. Besides I had to numb the pain within head and my heart. From that moment on, it was on and popping non-stop. East Cleveland was the place that I could drink and drug everyday all day. I am not proud to report that is just what I did for the next four years! I was living like I had lost my mind, because I had lost myself only I did not know it!

To get help you must first identify the problem exist. I just wasn't ready yet to admit that I needed help, So, I ran with people who were just like me...I had become a full-blown addict"

"If you never been to the pits of Hell, Thank God!"

Chapter 24

"The Nightmare Begins"

(Dealing with an untreated Dis-ease)

Adjusting to my addicted lifestyle was almost unbearable. Day after day. I sought ways to cope and forget my failures by using chemicals. I tried alcohol, marijuana, crack cocaine, and pills (black beauties). Taking pills were out of the question because I had a hard time swallowing those. Marijuana made me too sleepy to function, so I barely smoked weed. However, if that was all that was available, it worked. Alcohol went straight to my blood stream and crack cocaine afforded me to run around for days on end with minimal sleep, food, or self-care. I quickly moved from my apartment to the streets which I knew little about. I thought about going to Mommie's, but that meant following rules and being responsible and I was not ready for that. Living on the block meant adapting to street codes. "Six-Five" meant the police were coming. "Hooty-Hoot" meant somebody was looking for drugs. When a girl was strolling the streets that meant she was open for business. I hooked up with all the other drug users and dealers in East Cleveland. They appeared to like me and accepted me into their circle. I hooked up with a big dope dealer. In the beginning, I was still getting public assistance, so every first of the month; I was a loyal and trusted customer of the dope man. He made sure I had a place to stay and food to eat, but you know it was not free. I began to make other connections that led me away from him. For whatever reasons, he remained kind to me throughout my stay in East Cleveland. He began to tell me that I had to pay my own way after a while. You see, which meant I had to pull my own weight and my welfare checks had stopped because the kids were no longer with me. Eventually, I did not have a place to stay and my looks were completely gone!

The word was a girl could take the risk of selling her body to get dope money or she could risk going to jail for stealing from stores and sell merchandise to make her money to buy drugs. I actually had options to continue my drug use. No longer was my drug use an option. The choice became which chemical I was going to use each day to get "High." For me, my only option was numbing the pain of the "Nightmare" I lived every day for four years on the streets of East Cleveland.

I began to meet all kinds of people. Some of them genuinely liked me. Some of them hated me. I began to frequent parties and I even met a couple of people who came looking for me to spend big money with. I called those people my V.I.P customers. As crazy as it sounds, I had favor on the streets.

The devil will set you up for death. The only thing was when the drugs were gone; those thoughts came back about my failed marriage, and the loss of my children. I had been gone for years and I missed them. I missed my momma and family. I could not get high enough to forget that I used to live another lifestyle besides hanging in the streets. It began to hurt again and I longed for home. Every now and then, I would go home. I tried to stay but my addiction kept calling me back to the streets. Not to mention, I stole from my family to buy drugs and they hated me for that. I didn't blame them. I missed them and loved them so much, but I couldn't stop using drugs.

The last time I hit the streets, I hit the streets hard. I was meeting all kinds of folk and began stooping real low. I made promises to folk I could not keep. I got jumped by five girls and had a black eye for not buying drugs from one of their boyfriends. How stupid is that. I had a gun pointed at my head (two times) for not paying a dope man five dollars. Really? I went to jail four times for shoplifting. My life was shot to hell and my body was quickly following. I remember meeting an elderly couple who took to me and always treated me kind. They even asked me why was I living on the streets because I was not like the other girls. The wife told me to never forget that all I had to was go home and things would get better for me. I met a guy who was in recovery and one night he took me to an AA meeting. The people at the meeting were happy and they all greeted me with a "BIG" welcome. A gentleman shared his story of pain to victory and how he overcame his addiction to substance use "One Day At A Time." Ludicrous I thought when he was done. I left the meeting so I could get served, but I never forgot his story. I think it planted a seed of hope.

It became harder and harder to feed my addiction. People began to use and abuse me. When my money was gone, I had to hit the streets. I was no longer allowed in many stores and establishments and I had to travel further and further away to get merchandise to sell. I was tired and I became physically sick. I remember sleeping on a porch one night because nobody would let me in. It was snow on the ground and I stayed warm by taking all my clothes and putting them on top of my body. I promised God if I survived the cold, I would go home. The next day I went home, but I didn't stay. What was wrong with me? Why couldn't I stop destroying myself. What kept pulling me back into the black hole of despair and addiction. I began to pray and I thought about the apostle Paul and King David in the Bible. Their lives were less than perfect. If God could use them, surely, he could forgive and use me. I was bitter inside and nobody understood what I was going through not even me.

I remembered going to see Nina in the hospital after she had surgery. I walked in and she sat up in her bed with tears in her eyes. She said mommy people tell us you don't love us because of what you are doing. She said we don't know where you are and it is too much for us. Nina said I have people coming and I want you to leave. I do not want them to see you like this. That's when my Aunt Dena walked in and her mouth dropped. I never thought about the fact that I had stayed up the night before using drugs and crying because Mommie told me not to come to the hospital to see Nina because she didn't want her upset. I remembered going to visit the kids at Mommie's house and being asked to leave after 20 minutes because that was all I was allowed. That was crazy as hell to me. Those were my children. How dare they keep me away. I did what I knew to do, so I left and continued to use until I could no longer get high.

I was angry at all the wrong people. Why was I angry at the people who loved me and wanted the best for me? Why couldn't I see that they had to show me tough love to protect themselves. Besides, every time I came around, I stole from them and lied to them. I did just about anything I could to get a dollar to feed my addiction. I was hurting and no matter how high I got, the pain and the thoughts of what I lost would not go away. I know that God had his hand on me the whole time, because he kept sending me people and signs to encourage me. I was walking through one of the stores and I saw a picture of a black woman and a little boy. He was looking up at his momma. She had a big smile on her face and she had her eyes closed. The little boy was looking up smiling. The caption on the picture said, "I will always love my Momma." I stood there in the store and cried. I missed my children and I wanted to get them back. I didn't know how I was going to get them back, but I had to get them back. I began to pray and I told God I wanted to live again. I promised God that if he helped me make a brand-new start, I would stop using drugs and get my life together because I wanted and needed to be a Mommie again. One day it happened. I took a long hard look at my life and I surrendered. I was ready to do whatever I could to get sober. I walked away from that lifestyle of sex, crime, and drug use. In a moment of sanity, I decided to live. Nobody else was going to put me out. I was sick and tired of being sick and tired and I walked away from East Cleveland and never looked back. I walked to University Hospital and my Best friend (Angela) came and picked me up and took me to safety.

(She had to distance herself to protect herself, however, when I decided that I was ready to get help she was there for me)

(This is an example of tough love)

Chapter 25

"Recovery"

I will never forget that day as long I live. I was cold, sick, hungry, dirty, and tired. Not really knowing where I was going, but determined that today was the day for my life to change. As I walked, I thought about two people who told me that when I got ready to stop using drugs to give them a call. The first person I called was My best friend Angela. I told her that I was ready to get help. She asked me where I was and I told her I was walking down Euclid headed towards 105th streets. She told me to wait for her at University Hospital. When she saw me, she cried. I had lost a lot of weight and I was smelling like an out-house. I don't know how she endured my smell, but she did. All I could say was I was tired and I was ready to change. I told her that I had a male friend named Leon who told me he could get me into a treatment center. We went to her house and I ate and cleaned up. The clothes I had on had to be thrown away. Leon was at work when I called him. I asked him if he could help me get into that treatment center he told me about and he said yes. Leon talked with Angela and arranged for me to stay at her house until he could come and pick me up. I slept most of the day. Angela's parents Little Mommy and Mr. C. We're at home and they loved on me and encouraged me by telling me everything was going to be alright. Little Mommy told me she had been praying for me and she hugged me and started crying. I immediately felt the love of God in my heart and as I cried too, I knew that everything was going to be all right. Leon arrived later that night to pick me up and take me to Harbor Lights on Prospect Ave. Leon assured me that everything would be okay and he was proud of me for deciding to get help. He told me not to worry about food or clothes because the facility had everything that I would need. Besides, the only thing I owned was the clothes on my back that Angela had given me. I had a bag with a doll in it for Stephenie and a hat for Stephen III. The First thing I had to do was get an assessment. The counselor, Mr. Frank, could see the doll in my bag and he asked me why I had the doll. I told him it was for my daughter Stephenie. He laughed with a sigh of relief. He told me that he thought he was going to have to send me to the psych ward because it's not every day you see a grown woman walking around with a doll. He completed my assessment and shook my hand and wished me the best. I stayed at harbor lights for 14 days. My counselor was a Caucasian woman named Cindy. She asked me if I would be willing to go to a treatment facility after detox and I said yes. She asked me if I knew where Lorain was and Immediately said yes, because I Had cousins who lived on West 25th street. She laughed and said, no, I mean Lorain, Ohio. I said no. She informed me of a treatment facility in Lorain, Ohio that she had made arrangements for me to attend, if I was serious about getting sober. I told her that I was tired of living a lifestyle filled with drug use and I wanted to get my children back. I wanted to get my life back and became willing to do whatever was necessary for that to happen. I had a physical by the doctor and I was prescribed medication and vitamins to build up my immune system. I attended groups and meetings every day until a bed opened-up for me at the shelter in Lorain. I called Nina who was in college in Georgia at the time to tell her I was in treatment. She cried and said she was proud of me. I missed so many important events in her life and let her down so many times and to hear her so those words, instantly brought tears to my eyes. I called Stephenie and Stephen III to tell the news and they were so happy. My mother and mother in law encouraged me to stay focused and do whatever the people told me so I could get better and come home. I remember attending one of my last group meetings at the center and I remember the counselor, Mr. Frank saying, "never forget the pain, because if you forget the pain, you may go back." He also said "one out of every ten clients remain in recovery. I immediately counted the ten people in the room and said to myself he must be talking to me. I made a sober and conscious promise to God that l was going to get my life back. I was ready for this thing called "sobriety."

Chapter 26

"Lorain, Ohio"

Angela drove me to what would be my new home for the next 30 days or more until I Could get into alcohol and drug treatment. It was called the Hope Center. When I say, this place was packed with love and support for your every need, I mean it. The people their received me with open arms. This goes for the staff and the residents. There is nothing like coming inside and feeling love and warmth after being outside in the cold cruel world. The staff referred me to other agencies and connected me with the right people who could help me get financial assistance, housing, AA meetings, health care and everything in between. I met people from all walks of life who literally gave me the shirts off their backs. I signed up for housing because my goal was to get my children back. I contacted Mommie and let her know that I had safely arrived. She encouraged me to stay and get the help I needed to continue to stay sober. The donations came in weekly at the shelter and I began getting items for myself, my children and our new home. If I was planning on moving, I needed to get prepared and I took full advantage of the services offered to me.

I met some women and men in recovery that are still my friends today. One of the women took me to the church across the parking lot from the homeless shelter and I loved it.

I had an amazing experience at Morning Star Baptist Church. It reminded me of the church I grew up in back in Cleveland as a little girl. The pastor's name was Dr. Mark Ward III and his wife was Sis. Bonnie Ward who played the piano for the church and was also the minister of music. They had for awesome children around the ages of Stephenie and Stephen III. Their names were Mark lV, Adam, Joyce, and James. I met the secretary of the church named Sis. Sally Sharp and she became my God Mother and Guardian Angel. Sis. Sharp took me under her wing and her family helped me until I got on my feet and even after. I joined the church and remained an active member from 1999 until 2009. I sang in the choir, and sang with a special group of women named the "Voices of Praise" and taught vacation Bible school. Through prayer and lots of patience, the pieces of my broken life began to come together. I got a job at the temp agency until I could get into treatment. I am a firm believer in the statement that "idle hands are the devils workshop." I got active in church, AA meetings and work.

I met a woman at the homeless shelter who worked for the treatment facility to provide services to the shelters residents by the name of Pat Brown. She held AA meetings at the homeless shelter and met with me individually. She talked about addiction, sobriety, and the process of recovery. She connected me with a program called "Shelter Plus" which would allow me to get my own apartment. All I had to do was follow the instructions and remain a residence at the homeless shelter to qualify. I was determined to get my children back. After living on the streets of East Cleveland and being put out of everywhere, I finally decided to do whatever I had to do to get my life back. I remember telling Pat that I talked with my mom earlier that day about the children. I told her the children needed me and therefore, I was going back to Cleveland. Pat reminded me that the children needed me the whole time I was active in my addiction, and the only reason for my present concern was because I was sobering and I had begun to feel emotions again. Pat encouraged me to stay on Lorain and continue working on my recovery. She said that the disease of addiction was powerful, cunning and baffling and it would use anything and anybody to draw me back into my addiction. She encouraged me to get a sponsor and continue to go to meetings, so I did. I met a woman named Shirley who was in recovery at the homeless shelter. We were in room #5. Every morning and night she got on her knees and prayed. I asked her to be my sponsor and she began taking me to meetings with her and talking with me about recovery and the "Big Book" of Alcoholics Anonymous. She began taking me through the "12 Steps of Recovery." Shirley's favorite chapter in the Big Book was "How it Works." She would always say "Rarely have we seen a person fail who has thoroughly followed our path." She said I didn't have to be perfect; instead, I had to be willing to follow a few suggested steps. She asked me one question, "What are you willing to do stay sober?" I prayed to God for strength to live a sober life every day and he continued to connect me with the right people to help me do just that! Today, I know that God had a plan for my life when he sent me to Lorain, Ohio to reside at a homeless shelter, while I waited to get into Alcohol and Drug treatment that was across the parking lot from Morning Star Baptist Church.

Chapter 27

"Alcohol and Drug Treatment, AA meetings and Church"

Treatment was everything I was expecting it to be and then some. We were housed in a home by the park surrounded by trees. It was called the "Comfort House." It was breathtaking, serene, and quiet. It was everything I had not been used to in a long time, because it involved structure, boundaries, and accountability. A person who is "addicted" to chemicals basically does what they want, when they want, and how long they want. There is constant chaos in an addicted lifestyle. Addicts are focused on the temporary fix in life with no boundaries attached. Superficial relationships work best because there is no accountability involved. Addiction is about living life recklessly with a continual dependence on the use of a substances.

Recovery is about recovering all the things lost in addiction. The outlook on life changes as the addicted person's world becomes inundated with endless thoughts, plans, and goals for escaping reality, through the use of alcohol and drugs. What started out as fun, becomes a horror story. Lost relationships, financial and legal issues, mental and physical issues, as well as, countless other problems begin to engulf the life of the addicted person. Addicts are often filled with fear, guilt, shame and hopelessness about the current state of their lives. It is not until the addicted is introduced to a new way of life through abstinence, that they begin to find help and regain strength necessary to overcome the insurmountable negative circumstances they experience, as a result of their lives spiraling out of control as a result of their addiction. Until the addicted person surrenders to this new way of life, they will continue in the cycle of addiction. Everything in the addict's world must "CHANGE" if they are going to recover. The addicted person is the only one who can bring this to pass.

For me, without GOD, my recovery would have never been possible because after 18 days of being at the "Comfort House" I was asked to leave. I met a counselor who was about the business and she was not falling for my crap! I tried to take over group one day. My big mouth and addictive behaviors and unwillingness to change, allowed me to find myself on the outside looking in. Reality set in quickly and I was packing and leaving the safe haven called residential treatment. I found out fast that they were not willing to risk the other women in the house because I was unwilling to completely follow the rules. My counselor at the Comfort House (Sabrina) and the founder's wife (Cathy Frank) encouraged me to stay strong and keep working the program. They both assured me that I had what I needed to stay sober as I walked away not knowing where I was going. I had money saved from my last job and a check that was given to me at the time of my departure. I could have taken that opportunity of getting put out of treatment as the perfect reason to return to alcohol and drug use, but I wanted my sobriety. Something inside of me kicked into overdrive and screamed keep fighting. Don't sink, swim!!! In that moment, I wanted to stay sober like I need air to breath to stay alive!

For some reason, I did some of the things I was told when I was in the Comfort House and got numbers from sober women at the

AA meetings. I called the secretary at the church (Sis. Sally Sharp) and a sister that I met at an AA meeting who was a Christian (Carla) and explained to them the pickle I had gotten myself into. The secretary was willing to let me stay with her over night until my AA sister picked me up after she got off work the next day. I called my mom and let her know that I was put out of treatment; however, I planned to stay in Lorain. She encouraged me to stay focused on staying sober and staying away from negative people. She told me that everything happened for a reason and assured me that GOD still had a plan for my life. She also told me to do more listening and less talking. This reminded me of the saying "take the cotton out your ears and put it in your mouth." I believe this forced me to get serious about my sobriety and helped me to humble myself so GOD could continue to use me and reveal to me his plan for my life. I realized that my life is in GOD's hands and I had to get out of his way so he could work.

Looking back with hindsight, I feel a need to explain my addicted mindset when I was in treatment. First of all, some of the counselors were in recovery, so in my addicted mind, they were no better than I was, even though I was the one in treatment. Second of all, I was willing to listen to them talk about recovery and change; however, I was not willing to let them to teach me how recovery works. Lastly, after treatment closure for the girls in the house, I was holding Bible study in my room. When the monitors came by the rooms after group everybody surrounded my bed with their bibles. I also used my cosmetology skills to do the ladies nails from 1:00-2:00pm after lunch and hair between the hours of 5:00-6:00pm before meetings at night. And to top it all off, I had a bad attitude! REALLY! That was until I met a counselor named Tammy Fields. It took 20 minutes of my stuff and she had me packing and on the curb. This was sobering in a different kind of way. The whole time I was in treatment they kept telling me that the recovery is a program of change. Recovery is not for those who need it, but rather it was for those who wanted it. I can still hear these words of truth "If nothing changes, Nothing Changes!

"Insanity is doing the same thing over and over again, expecting to get a different result"

I remember saying a prayer and walking up route 254. I felt one foot hit the curb and the other land in the palm of God. He has been leading and guiding me every step of the way.

Chapter 28

"Returning to my first Love, God"

Carla picked me up the next morning from Sis. Sharp's house and took me back to the Hope Center to see if I could be readmitted to the shelter for additional housing. The staff informed me that I could come back after 30 days. It had only been 19 days and I had approximately two weeks to go to reach the 30day mark. Carla let me stay with her. As bad as I thought things were, God began to show me favor. That night Carla took me to church with her and my life has never been the same. She was Hispanic and attended a Spanish speaking church. The service was amazing and the Spirit of God could be felt in the church. The preacher would preach in Spanish and the church would say "amen." Carla would interpret the message and then I would say "amen." Then Carla started shouting and I was standing there looking lost. Nevertheless, I could feel the love for the Lord in my heart. At the end of the service, Pastor Foster called me forward and prophesied over me. He put his hands on his hips and said, "Did you know that you will be working with children in the future?" I laughed to myself and thought he must not know that I don't even have my own children with me. Nevertheless, I received his words. Carla explained my situation to him and he prayed for me in English. This was truly the beginning of my new life in Christ. I received the blessing of the Holy Spirit.

I went back to work for the Temp Agency and began to work again in factories. I continued to attend AA meetings and began to look for a sponsor as suggested in AA to help me go through the 12 Steps. I reunited with Morning Star Baptist Church. Sis Sharp picked me up for church until I was eligible to move back into the Hope Center, which was right next door to Morning Star. I can truly say that through prayer and patience, God began to open new doors for me to walk through. God turned a bad situation into a blessing once I got out of the way. I resumed singing in the choir; l joined a woman's gospel group called "The Voices of Praise" under the direction of pastor Ward's wife, Sis Bonnie Ward. I loved attending Sunday School. My Sunday School teacher Teresa Little and her mother Dottie Bowers were steeped in the word of God and both were anointed by God to teach the word. Everything I needed to continue in my recovery began to materialize.

"I found out that God does not need my help, rather I shall for the rest of my life continually need his"

"They always encouraged me to get out of the way and let God work"

Chapter 29

"Lord Please Restore Me"

I eventually moved back into the Hope Center and resumed working with the counselor Pat Brown. She encouraged me to attend AA meetings and get a Sponsor. She reminded me that I had signed up for the "Shelter Plus Program" which would allow me to get my own place so my children could come back home with me. She said I was fourth on the list. She encouraged me to stay on the sober path and not get into any trouble because it would all be worth it in the end. I continued to work at the temp agency. I was blessed to save money and take care of my personal needs.

I began going to Cleveland to visit my children and family. I met this guy one night at an AA meetings that was such a nice gentleman, but I told myself that I did not have time for that and quickly dismissed the thought of starting a relationship. One night after work, I got a message upon returning to the Hope Center that everyone who was not on the "Shelter Plus" list had to leave the Center. This is what I call God doing for me what I couldn't do for myself. Pat Brown informed us that we had to attend AA meetings daily at the center, work, and stay sober evidenced by us passing random UDS. The thought of me having my own place and getting my children back was a dream I longed to see come true. Miraculously, I lived at the "Hope Center" for 5 months. The staff told me I lived there longer than anyone in their history of working at the center. I continued to pray, stay in touch with Mommie and my children, work, attend AA meetings and attend church. I even got another sponsor (Janice Palmers) to take me through the first 166 pages in the AA Big Book. I was also allowed to participate in the "After Care" treatment program at the men's Comfort House and my counselor was the incredible Tommy Ward! He whistled a lot and said things like "We are as sick as our secrets and the very thing that we hide is the very thing that could make us return to alcohol or drug use. That's all I needed to hear because I began to share my story with others! Tommy said if you want to keep your sobriety, you must give it away. He remained a big part of my recovery and is a true inspiration to me.

That's when it happened! I was informed by the "Hope Center" staff that everyone living at the center for more than 30 days had two weeks to evacuate the premises. This included the people on the "Shelter Plus" program. Took the wind right out of me! What was I going to do now? I was informed by Pat Brown that l was second on the list for housing. I reached out to the people at church and in the AA program. I began to pray day in and day out. My church friends encouraged me to keep praying. My AA friends encouraged me to stay sober. With one week to go, I attended an AA discussion meeting at the Central Office and shared my housing situation.

An AA friend named Youseff, took me up the street to the offices of Sterling and Janice Palmers. They had their own business and helped connect people in AA to housing, employment, mental health and human services agencies. I told them that I would be homeless in 7days and l would have to stop working at the temp agency if I didn't find somewhere to go.

The funny thing was that l had met the Palmers at the "Hope Center." I asked Janice Palmers to sponsor me and after one look at me she said no. God has a way of giving us what we need, when you need it and for me, he did just that. The Palmers found me vouchers to pay for 10 days at the Journey Inn Motel. I felt a sigh of relief knowing that God blessed me with additional housing. Sis. Sally Sharp and her family continued to help me no matter what happened or where I had to go.

I remember finally calling mom and telling her about the housing issues. Mommie encouraged me to stay in Lorain. She knew that l was doing the best l had done in a long time and she did not want me to mess it up by returning home. Although, Mommie new nothing about the AA program, her discerning Spirit told her that I could make it Lorain. I attended an AA meeting two days before l was scheduled to leave the Motel. The lady (Deidra) that chaired the meeting was the person who spoke at the first lead meeting l attended after entering treatment. In "AA" they say "A problem shared, is a problem cut in half. I shared my housing dilemma with Deidra and she informed that the "Lorain County Mission" had just opened its doors in Elyria to provide housing for those in need. All I can say is "Glorrrrrrrrrrrrry"! God may not come when we want him but he is always on time.

God blessed me to be accepted into the Mission family. Apostle Byron Walters, his wife Pastor Hope Walters, his two sons Byron Jr. and Mark and their daughter Breon lived there, along with other tenants at the mission. I was the second female to enter the Mission, however, l was the first female alcoholic. After the intake process, l called Mommie to let her know that I would be staying at the Mission until my housing unit became available. Every day was filled with Bible study and other church events.

The only drawback was not being able to attend Morning Star Baptist Church. I informed Sis. Sally about this and she told me that the church was praying for me and encouraged me to keep the faith. My Spirituality and knowledge in the Word of God began to grow in ways that l cannot explain. I met Georgia Williams and Cathy Williams who facilitated bible study and other programming at the Mission. I also met Apostle Chase Higgins and his wife Pastor Virginia Higgins who became my spiritual brother and sister in Christ. I learned about fasting, prayer, and worship. I watched God bless me in ways that I can barely find words to explain. I am eternally grateful to Apostle Walters and his wife and his children's, as well as, their other family members sacrifice and labor of love. They were willing to share all they had to give to those of us who are less fortunate and answer the call of God over their lives.

(Apostle Byron knew his assignment to help the homeless and God sent him and his family for such a time as this to open the Lorain County Mission...Somebody say PURPOSE)

Chapter 30

Staying Focused through Prayer!!!

I remained at the Mission until my apartment through the "Shelter Plus" program was ready. This took about 2 months. I learned that praying is useless, if you are going to give up. The People in AA told me to stay focused, clean house, and trust GOD if I was going to succeed. The people in church told me to "Let Go and Let God." God showed me incredible favor and I continued attending AA meetings from the Mission. I began to meet numerous of anointed spiritual leaders in Lorain County throughout my stay at the Mission. It was prophesied by Pastor Gains that I would be working with men. Minister Janice palmer prophesied that I would be working with women.

I joined the Missions praise team and continued to use my musical gifts to glorify God. As I look back, I know that God intervened on my behalf by placing me at the Mission. I remember Dr. Ward of Morning Star Baptist Church preaching the sermon "If It Does not exist, God will create It! I took it personally and connected it to "The Lorain County Mission." When I came to Lorain in 1999, the Mission did not exist. I believe that God is always working behind the scene on our behalf and sometimes all we must do is stay focused and keep praying! I remember getting a call from my ex-husband complaining about our children and making threats about me coming to get them. It messed me up and through off my square. Sis. Georgia Williams saw me crying and immediately took me into her office. She anointed me with oil and prayed me under a desk. She reminded me that I was going to fight the enemy through "prayer" for the rest of my life and that's exactly what I began to do. "Pray, Pray, and Pray" became my model. I also adapted the term "PUSH" which stands for "Pray Until Something Happens." I became a "Prayer Warrior."

The time at the Mission passed quickly and after a couple of months, my apartment was ready. I was so excited and I felt extremely blessed and highly favored by God. The women at the Mission (Georgia Williams, Carol Williams, and Pastor Hope) got together and gave me a house warming party. My favorite gift was a "Recovery Bible". I would read all day and all night until I fell asleep. The truth is, if you want to get to know somebody, try spending time with them. I truly began to fall in love with Jesus. I spent as much time as I could, reading the Bible. I continued to grow in the word of God. Everything I needed God supernaturally provided. Clothes, food, shelter and even furniture for my home was provided for me through the Mission. I was going to miss attending daily bible studies and evening services once I moved. I talked with Apostle and Pastor Walters about my concerns about leaving the Mission. They assured me that I received what I needed to move forward in my life. They encouraged me to stay focused and keep praying! My granny's words came back to my mind when she said, "God will give you a family" and that is exactly what he did through Apostle Byron, his wife Pastor Hope and the staff and residents at "The Lorain County Mission."

Chapter 31

"Another Level"

Moving into my own place after being homeless for years was a dream comes true. Every time I went into my home and shut the door I would get down on my knees and pray. I worked hard to practice the teachings I learned at the Mission. I went back to Morning Star Baptist Church. Sis Sally picked me up for church and Bible study weekly. I went back to work through the temp agency and resumed attending my AA meetings. I did everything I could think of to stay sober. And then it happened!!! My ex-husband called and threatened me again to come and get the children. I wanted to, but the clause in the contract through "Shelter Plus" was for me only to occupy the apartment. I shared that with him and he was not having it. He even called me a part time mother. Hurt was an understatement for how I felt. It appeared that every prayer and positive thing I learned and practiced led me to this moment. It appeared that my world turned upside down. So, I did what I know to do and l called the prayer warriors at the church and the Mission and l fasted and prayed for 24 hours. I went to a Bible study and prayer meeting, and a AA discussion group and shared my problems with people who supported me. Within the next three days my aunt Dena and uncle Karl called me and told me they would take the children until l got a place for us to live. I Love aunt Dena and uncle Karl. I shared this news with Pat Brown and she signed me up for section 8. And guess what, l was approved. All l had to do now was wait for a place to become available before we could move in. These are just some of the reasons that I tell everybody, anywhere, that "Prayer" still Works!!!

Waiting was not easy. I still had to work, attend church and AA meetings and pray. I continued to avoid using people and using places. I continued to meet with my children on the weekend in Cleveland by Greyhound. I was having dinner with an AA friend and I mentioned getting a car. He informed me that he had a car that he had gotten for someone else and they were not paying the bill. He said if they missed another payment the car could be mine. Up until that point my support system was incredible at picking me up for church, AA meetings, work and shopping. I prayed and asked God where my car was as suggested by my childhood friend Kyle. Within one week l was driving my own car. Can you hear the music? I danced for the whole entire service when I got to church that Sunday. Having my own car meant being responsible for myself. I enjoyed taking myself to church, work, and meetings and to visit my children. Pat Brown encouraged me to pick them up and let them visit on the weekends until my three-bed room housing unit became available. My Mommie was so proud of me! She still had no clue about the purpose of AA meetings, sponsors or Recovery Coins. Mommie even asked if I could spend my AA anniversary coin! I told her no, and encouraged her not to ask another AA member that question. The truth is that Mommie does not have to understand any of those things, rather, l must. All she knew is whether it was AA, CA, NA or any other support group or self-help group, she finally had her daughter back.

Things continued to progress in positive ways in my life. However, living life on life's terms meant being ready for the unexpected. That's what happened when my Aunt and Uncle called and informed me that they could no longer keep Stephen and Stephenie. I did what l know to do and begin to pray. I contacted my sponsor and went to church and AA meetings. Regardless to the opposition I faced, God continued to rain down his favor in my life and my little ones went to live with their father's mother (Adaline Tiggs). She assured me that she would keep the children until my housing unit was approved and that's just what she did. I Love Adaline Tiggs!!! God continued to show me his mercy and grace by keeping me safe and my children safe until we resumed our lives as a family!

Chapter 32

"Reunited"

I got off work one day and received a call from the housing agency that our apartment was ready and we could move in at any time. Joy is all l felt in my soul! Everything l was taught about prayer and the promises in AA were coming true. I am a believer that God may not come when you want him, but he is always on time. Our apartment was a brand-new unit. We were the first family to occupy it. The children were finally home and enrolled in their new schools. Nina was grown and she was doing okay in her own church, working, and living in her own place.

We eventually moved into a brand-new single-family home with a huge front and back yard, with a full front porch. I continued to work at JLC and took vacations with children and was blessed to take them on numerous family outings. We became active in the church, the choir, and Sunday School. I got my first SUV and continued to visit with my mother and other family members in Cleveland.

I got married to a wonderful man of God named Donnie Carter from West Virginia. When I first met him, he was a little too fly for me. He wore colors like red, lime green and his favorite was orange. I thought to myself, l don't think so, but God had others plans. After getting to know him, I found out that he was a perfect gentleman. I am happy to report that has never changed. He is a truck driver and loves to travel and see the world. He even liked music and had worked with some of the same phenomenal people I worked with in my music career. He had a beautiful daughter named Debra who passed away three years after we were married. Donnie's family has accepted me as their own and l love them all. My children liked Donnie and he took excellent care of us. God gave me what l needed when he blessed me with Donnie. We have a lot of fun together alone and with the children. I Love you Donnie and you are the wind beneath my wings.

When you merge two families it is difficult and even trying at times, however, through prayer and not giving up, you can survive it. I have learned to ask the right questions when l need answers. I have also accepted the fact that parents are not perfect and we sometimes make mistakes. However, there is an order in the home and that is God first, husband, wife and then children. I have also learned that when I was single there was an order in my life and that was God first and then me! If I cannot take care of me, I cannot take care of anybody else! Donnie always encouraged me to take care of myself and my children. The Bible says in Proverbs 18:22 "He who finds a wife finds a good thing and obtains favor from the Lord." I am glad that Donnie agrees with me that "As for me and my house, we will serve the LORD" (Joshua 24:15).

Please remember "A house divided cannot stand" (Mark 3:25).

"We have to find a way in the family unit to keep everybody on the same page through consistency and communication"

Chapter 33

"My life today"

Due to my remaining sober and letting God lead and direct my path, I have witnessed miracle after miracle in my life. Nobody could have put my life back together like this, but God.

Nina is a minister/author/motivational speaker/aroma therapist who is married to a wonderful man named Kenneth Worthington. Stephenie has a Bachelors' Degree in Music from Kent State and is a Music teacher and is engaged to Ronald Lawson. Stephen III is in the Air force and is married to Veronica Rosario and they have blessed us with two handsome grandsons Donnell 5 years old (Named after my husband Donnie) and Carlton 15 months. We have continued to grow together in the word of God as a family.

I was reunited with my father and his wife (Joanne) and two brothers (Karl and Kenton) and two sisters (Sherry and Sheryl) and a slew of nieces and nephews that l met in 2013. I have been blessed to have the privilege of developing a relationship with my father. I can truly say that no matter how long it may take, Prayer works! If it is Gods will for you, nothing or nobody can stop his plan. My Aunt Dena, Uncle Karl and Momma Vivian (Nina's grandma) have all passed away! My goals are to live my life victoriously through Christ so that their labor of love and sacrifices towards me and my children will never be in vain. To my Queen, l LOVE You Mommie and words could never express how much you mean to me. Thank you for your unconditional love!!! Family means everything.

I went back to school and received an Associate Degree in Human Services (age 49), a Bachelor's Degree in Theology (age 54), and l am currently pursuing my Master's Degree as a Licensed Professional Counselor (age 55). I am an Associate Minister and Youth Minister at our church since in 2013. I teach Sunday School for adolescents and l am the Director of the Youth Choir. I want to say thank you to my Pastor and church family for helping me grow into a Servant of God. Pastor your unselfish love for Gods people is evident in the way you feed Gods sheep! Continued Blessings!

I am currently an Adolescent Chemical Dependency Counselor. I believe that due to the destruction I caused in my own children's lives, God has anointed and appointed me to help youth overcome inevitable difficulties and obstacles that are sure to come in life. It is my desire to live, sing, and shout to the Glory of God for the Wonderful things he has done in my life.

I still have a bucket list of things to accomplish and if it is Gods will, it's all mines!

"In Closing"

As I look back over my life, the damage of my "Addicted" lifestyle affected my children in unhealthy ways. If I had it to do all over again, I would. I will never know all that I missed not being there to watch them grow up. We were separated for a total of seven years. Four of those years were due to my addiction and three were spent in recovery working on myself. Trying to recover the things that were lost in my addiction was the hardest part. No one will ever know the pain, guilt, and shame I felt not having my children in my life for all those years. It was not easy facing each day with people constantly treating you less than because of your past mistakes. Staying focused by praying and keeping God first in my life, attending church, and AA meetings, and surrounding myself with positive people who supported my recovery kept me on the right path. Some days things got so bad that all I could do was pray and cry out to God for help. Nevertheless, l am grateful for every issue, test and trial, every tear l shed, and every prayer l prayed because it made me into the woman l am today. God took my pain and mistakes and shaped me into his vessel so he could use my story, to help somebody else. l am grateful that God continues to keep his promises to me. I am grateful for my family, friends and church family's continued support. I am forever grateful for the AA program, the AA fellowship, and the 12 steps of recovery.

Prayer is the Key and Faith Unlocks the Door!

When All Else Fails, Pray and Trust God!

I Guarantee You, Prayer Still Works!!!

LaPhenie Joyce Bridges-Cloyd

(DestinyDrivenLC)

Additional Words...

Revealing, brute honesty, as she chronicles the events of her life from addiction to destiny. She gives a vivid account of each event in her life that moved her to where she is today. She holds nothing back. You can feel the struggles, disappointments, pain, and joys from beginning to end. She exposes her hurts, sorrows, and insecurities that God used to shape and mold her into whom He designed her to become. She shares her inner struggles, as well as her struggles with family, friends, and those not friends.

Her love and concern for family connection and her children are revealed; and abuse from the past, with feelings of not being good enough is exposed. A chain of unfortunate events led her down the road to her addiction to lessen and tune out the emotional and psychological pain from spousal abuse. But it was her love for her children that moved her to fight for them; to set herself free from her unwholesome past by drawing on the power of her faith in God. Prayer moved her to draw on the faithfulness of the God that her grandmother instilled in her.

This book is a must read for anyone who feels that there is no way out of a difficult situation. It offers insights to someone who believes that they have no options, and are on the verge of giving up. Further, her story will encourage you to never give up on yourself and your faith in God. This is a book of struggles, but it is also one of victory that refused to give into defeat no matter the number of times defeat and discouragement walked in.

This book further challenges you to consider carefully the choices you make in life and the consequences of your choices. Finally, this book shows what can happen to a life that is surrendered to the will and purpose of God.

Her story will inform and cause you to become more sensitive regarding the struggles and setbacks that others encounter in their lives.

This is a must-read story that reveals God's glory.

Rev. Dr. Shirley Ann Howard

"You meant it for evil..." These were the words of Joseph as he came face to face those who meant him harm, but God used those circumstances for his ultimate good. In this personal and compelling memoir, Minister LaPhenie Cloyd takes the reader on a journey of descent into the abyss of addiction. Her story begins as one who was designed to shine brightly and make her mark on the gospel music stage. Gifted by God with a raw talent that was destined to be used for His glory, like Joseph her destiny was designed with a downward detour. But like Joseph, her story provides the reader with divine evidence that although one can experience detours in life but that does not mean one's destiny has been derailed. Her life testifies to the truth that with God, you cannot judge a person's destiny by what it looks like in the moment. Even though from outward appearances it may looked like her destiny has been derailed, she allows us to see that when one has a relationship with God, no matter where you find yourself, you are still on track.

The author shares with us how, the enemy maneuvers his way into her life in to attempt to derail her through the sin of domestic violence. She experiences the loss of her marriage, the loss of her children, the loss of her family, the loss of herself and ultimately the loss of her song. You meant it for evil.... but God! God uses the challenges of marital abuse, drug addiction, loss of family and loss of self to bring her to the place of her destiny. Through her loss, God uses her to bring life to others. Through her pain, God uses her to reveal his promise that he will never leave you or forsake you. Through her brokenness God uses her to bless others with a powerful testimony of the transforming power of the Holy Spirit. Yes, what the enemy meant for evil.... was her addiction which was designed to kill her. God uses for good, for her addiction led to her destiny as she leads others out of the abyss of addiction that leads to death and into the promise of new life in Christ. This book will be a blessing to those who believes there is no way out of their addiction and no possibility for transformation in their lives. The enemy may have meant it for evil but through a relationship with Jesus it can lead to your destiny.

Rev. Marilyn Parker-Jeffries, Mapt

ABOUT THE AUTHOR

LaPhenie Joyce Bridges Cloyd Born January 5, 1962 is a native of Cleveland, Ohio. She is married to her loving husband Darrell Franklin Cloyd and is the Mother of Niyia Latrese, Sharmayne Nichole, and Sherman Thomas III. She is the grandmother of 5-year-old Darrelle Carmelo and 17-month-old Caleb Nehemiah.

LaPhenie began Singing gospel music at age of 5. She had her first concert age of 13 at United Missionary Baptist Church. At age 14, She began acting and has performed in multiple community plays such as "The Wiz that Is," "Pinocchio Live," "Shuffled Up, Decked Out, Alice", and "Until the Vinegar Runs Out." She won the "Best New Performers Award for her performance in "Tambourines to Glory and H.M.S Pinafore" at

Karamu for the "84-85" season. She is a founding member of "The Twilights of Joy" and His Inspirational Singers of Cleveland, Ohio." She has sung with numerous Choirs, groups, and bands in Greater Cleveland and Lorain, as well as recorded with various local artist. She was licensed as a cosmetologist March 21, 1985. She is an Honor graduate of Travel and Tourism 1993 (Atlanta Georgia).

My current work is a Chemical Dependency Counselor for Adolescents and their families. I love the work I do with the children. My goal is to have a positive impact on the decisions and choices they make for their future. I believe that children will rise to the expectations and standards set for them, if given the opportunity and chance to change. Although, the work is extremely challenging at times, I believe that working with the Adolescent population is where I am supposed to be.

She is currently the Youth Minister at New Creation Baptist Church under the leadership of Rev. Marilyn Parker-Jeffries. She received an Associate degree in Human Services at the University of Phoenix and a bachelor degree in (Theology) Christian studies with a concentration in youth ministry from Grand Canyon University. LaPhenie is currently pursuing her Master Degree as a Licensed Professional Counselor from Grand Canyon University.

LaPhenie's mission is to help people (especially Youth) overcome the inevitable barriers and obstacles that would prevent them from fulfilling their dreams and goals in life.

Made in the USA
Columbia, SC
26 May 2019